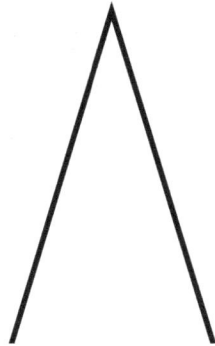

AuditionCraft

For Film & TV

The Craft, The Mastery, The Reality

By Linda Darlow

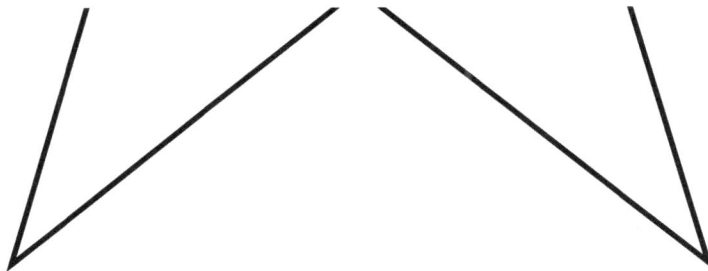

Foreword by John Noble

Artwork by Jasika Nicole

Produced by

FriesenPress

Suite 300 – 852 Fort Street
Victoria, BC, Canada V8W 1H8
www.friesenpress.com

Distributed to the trade by The Ingram Book Company

This book is dedicated to all of

my past, present and future students

who have been, are, and will be

my inspiration!

Respect For Acting
Uta Hagen

Acknowledgments

Writing this book was the easy part thanks to Michael Shurtleff's, *Audition.* His book became the basis for my film and television audition technique over 30 years ago. Thanks to my students who have helped me formulate, refine and clarify my audition technique, as well.

Getting it in print has been the hard part. I would not have been able to do it without the support of friends and colleagues, especially **P. Lynn Johnson** for her proof-reading skills and **Althea Kaye** for her editing expertise. Thank you also to Casting Director **Sid Kozak,** and Author and Acting Teacher **Carole Tarlington** for their feedback and suggestions.

I allowed a few others to read a draft of this book and must thank Director/Actor **Kristopher Tabori**, High School Film/Drama Department Head **Jim Crescenzo**, Actresses **Georgina Haig** and **Sarah Jane Redmond**, for their over-the-moon enthusiasm and encouragement. Their support has given me the courage to move forward with this project.

And a very special *Thank you* to those people who have actually physically contributed to these pages. **John Noble**, a brilliant actor and educator in his own right, for doing me the honor of writing such a lovely *Foreword.* **Jasika Nicole**, a triple-threat performer and talented artist, for her cover design and drawings. **Geoffrey Redknap**, a gifted writer/producer/director, for allowing me to use his scripts. **Henry Mah**, a talented writer/actor/teacher, for allowing me to use his script material as well as supporting everything else I do, and the lovely Casting Director, **Judy Lee,** for supplying some audition forms.

I must thank my daughter, **Leigh Ann**, for her patience, understanding, and accepting that I'm happier when I'm working – love you!

Foreword

Ask yourself.
Did you choose this acting business because you have unquenchable love for the craft?
Because you can't imagine a more fulfilling profession?
Because this is your passion?
If you answered "yes" to these questions then read on.

This book provides brilliant insights into how to approach the uncomfortable but critical hurdle of auditioning, specifically for film and television.

Linda Darlow has compressed a lifetime of experience as a first rate actor and teacher into this excellent guide.

This is the first book I have seen which provides the actor so clearly with the basic and essential elements of audition preparation.

What are sides? How do I break down character descriptions? What can I expect in the audition room? How should I prepare?

Obvious, perhaps, but rarely taught in such a matter-of-fact and assessable manner.

I have been associated with Linda for several years. She was my excellent dialect coach for 4 seasons of "Fringe". She is wise and witty and very perceptive. She tells it as it is without ever indulging in the doomsday warnings we so often encounter. She knows, as do I, that the path is strewn with difficulties, rejections and disappointments. But she never suggests that these hardships should douse our enthusiasm and passion. It is passion that has kept me in the business for 40 years as it has been for Linda.

I wish this book had been available to me when I was starting out in the business. I have made all of the mistakes she counsels against, and, like so many of my colleagues have had to sift through a minefield of conflicting opinions, techniques and approaches. I had to find my way stumbling in the dark. This book is a beacon to guide all actors from beginners to seasoned veterans.

Read the wisdom, take what helps you, grow in confidence, take your very best game into every audition, and walk away knowing you have served yourself and your craft well.

Let your passion win the day, every day.

John Noble

John Noble – *best known for his role as Dr. Walter Bishop on the TV Series, "Fringe" and his performance as Denethor in "The Lord of the Rings" Trilogy, John has an extensive list of Film & TV credits. An educator as well, John was Head of Drama at Brent School of Arts in Sydney as well as Artistic Director of Stage Company of South Australia.*

Contents:

Introduction

Our job as actors is to make what we do look easy – it isn't; actors who are serious about having a career, spend years studying, training and learning the skills of the trade. We take basic acting, scene study, improvisation, voice and movement classes. We study Shakespeare and the classics, theatre history, script analysis, singing, pantomime and dance – anything to improve our performance ability. We don't mind doing all of that because performing is our passion, an outlet for our creativity and self-expression. We spend a lot of time and money to become professional actors; to book that plum role that shoots us to stardom. And to get there most of us need to go through what is known in the business as "the audition".

Years ago, film and TV auditions were done live – there were no cameras. Auditions for commercials were also live. It wasn't until the advent of VHS and portable camcorders that the idea to tape auditions came into play and since then, DVD has replaced VHS tape. Though it doesn't change many of the basics of good acting, it does change almost *all* of the fundamentals and logistics of an audition.

My own career as an actress has spanned both eras, with and without camera. I have experienced every type of audition from Broadway stage, to commercials, to film & TV; I have also been a casting director, reader, producer, and stand-in. As an actress, I've done one-liners, actor and principal roles, guest star roles and supporting leads; but I didn't really start booking jobs until I mastered my own audition technique. Before I figured out how to do it, I really didn't like auditioning; now I love doing them and I book jobs.

Michael Shurtleff wrote the definitive book on the subject. Simply titled, *Audition*, it was published in 1978 and is still popular. I use his Guideposts in my own acting technique and in my classes, but Mr. Shurtleff's background and perspective was theatre. The book was published thirty years ago. Times have changed.

I developed my audition technique by incorporating, adjusting and distilling Mr. Shurtleff's wisdom into the logistics of acting and auditioning for camera. I began teaching it 25 years ago. I've written this book so that past, present and future students can have good notes to remind themselves, refresh their skills, and guide them through the arduous task of auditioning. This is a workbook, a *How-To* manual. It is my hope that this book will help make auditioning something you look forward to, not something you dread; it may take practice but it will come.

Section I, *The Craft of Auditioning*, details Mr. Shurtleff's 12 Guideposts, as well as other elements useful in preparing audition material. You may be surprised at how much information there is but I guarantee it will be helpful.

Section II, *The Mastery of Auditioning*, gives you insights into how this business of auditioning is handled and how you should prepare for the task. It will take you step by step through the process, from preparing at home to when it's over. This advice will allow you to be confident in taking charge in the audition room and help you enjoy your auditions.

Section III, *The Reality of Auditioning*, is about what it takes to make your dreams come true and how to handle your well-being as you pursue this career. It is important to have a realistic perspective on the business and maintain a healthy attitude regardless of the ultimate results.

In this book, as in my classes, my goal is to help you see auditioning as a necessary skill and to give you the tools to develop that skill as part of your craft. I want you to be able to approach your auditions with confidence, eagerness and a sense of mastery that will allow you to not only do your best, but also allow you to enjoy the process. After all, you will be spending as much, if not more, time auditioning then you will working.

Throughout this book I have used the generic term, actor, to mean both actor and actress.

Wishing you much success and joy in learning your craft and living your career!

Linda Darlow

~~~~~~~~~~~~~~~~~~~~~~~~~~~~~~~~~~~~~

Section One: The Craft of Auditioning

CHAPTER 1

Materials:

When you finally get that call for an audition, you will also get materials for it:

- A character breakdown
- The "sides"
- Possibly the whole script

Here's what to do with them:

THE BREAKDOWN (what it is)

It's a list of the characters with a description of who they are and what they're like. It may tell you the gender, age range, and what they do in the story if it's a short one. If it is detailed, it will give you physical qualities, personality type, and behavioral inter-relationship information.

NOTE:

A breakdown is created as a guideline – a place to start – in defining what type of actor they are looking for. It may be created by a casting director who has read the script. It can come from a consultation between: the writer, the director, the producer, the casting director. Its purpose is to help the casting director sort out which actors to bring in for each role. *The descriptions are not written in stone.* Occasionally, the descriptions change between sending out the breakdowns and the initial readings. The casting director will make the adjustments in choosing whom to bring in, but may not make the changes to the written breakdown. There is the possibility that the breakdown you get is inaccurate or will change in the casting process.

Sample: **Officer #1**, male, age 30 – 35, tall, large frame, tough, no nonsense, ACTOR ROLE

Sister Theresa, age 50 - 60, the cook, sweet but spunky, sense of humor, PRINCIPAL ROLE

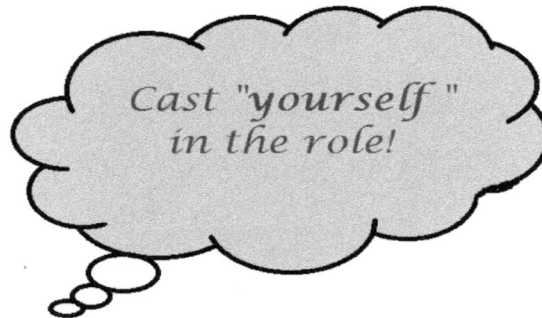

Cast "yourself" in the role!

THE BREAKDOWN (what to do with it)

If you get the breakdown for *all* the characters, read them all. There is valuable information in them about the plot line, the relationships, whom the character is talking to and whom he/she may be talking about. This is very helpful particularly when you have not been given the full script.

You may, however, only get the breakdown for your character and a short synopsis of the story line. Read the information, but remember that this description was created as a guideline only. After reading it, immediately *cast yourself in the role* whether or not you think it suits you.

If the description doesn't fit you but the casting director has invited you to audition for it, *you* are right for the role. Don't imagine someone else playing this part and then try to become that someone whom you're not. Don't play your judgment of that type of person either. For instance, if the role is that of a police officer, you think you have to be tough or up tight; or the role is of a nun so you think you have to be proper and angelic. Instead ask yourself, ***"How would I be if I were a cop or a nun?"***

THE SCRIPT: (what it is)

The script is a draft of the full story. It might be an early draft, close to a final or production draft, or something in between. The final draft won't happen until close to the start of filming; and even then, the color-coded revisions start to flow.

THE SCRIPT: (what to do with it)

Read the full script if you have access to it before your audition. There is always something to learn about what's going on and how your character fits into the story. It may not be anything you need to *play* in your scene, but you'll have a much better understanding of the overall tone, rhythm, pace and timing of the piece. You'll have more information regarding what your character is like, such as: background, relationships, past events, present situations, etc.

NOTE:

If you're reading for a TV Series that is already on the air, watch a few episodes, or check out information about that show on the Internet.

I know it sounds funny, but part of our job in this business is to watch television. You should know what shows are shooting in your area and have watched them at least once. You may not have time when you do get an audition to catch an episode or search the Internet.

The Internet is a good resource particularly for popular shows that have an extensive following. If you are reading for one of the Sci-Fi Series you may need to research the backstory and language for that world.

When you've seen some episodes or looked at the websites, you're better prepared to audition for the show. You know the look, the tone, the acting style. You know whether it's a light or dark comedy, or if it's drama. You will know when it takes place: the past, present or future. You will have a sense of the clothing, hair and make-up styles. So do yourself a favor and be on top of these shows beforehand, rather than scrambling at the last minute.

THE SIDES (what they are)

The sides are the scenes you will be performing in the audition. They are usually taken directly from the script, but could also be scenes created just for the purpose of the audition.

You should read *every bit* of writing on the page. Even the *page number* is useful. It tells you where in the story line this scene takes place.

This also means reading any parts of other scenes that might be on your pages. There may be some useful information there as well. If nothing else, it will inform you whether or not the *start* and *stop* in your scene has been accurately marked.

A list of abbreviations and terminology frequently used in script pages will help you fully understand the vision the writer has for the scene. You should have a working knowledge of this terminology so you know how to read everything on the page and understand what it means.

Some of the information is not something you need to do anything about but it is helpful to know.

You may come across terminology or abbreviations that aren't listed here. If you don't know what something means, ask someone or look it up. There are reference books available on this topic.

Following the Script Terminology are examples of how sides are marked by a casting director, with notes on how to follow those markings. There are also examples that will demonstrate issues to look out for when working with sides.

Script Terminology

INT = Interior
EXT = Exterior
VO/V.O. = Voice Over (and may or may not appear)
OS/O.S. = Off Screen (and may or may not appear)

Camera Terminology

CU = Close Up, **ECU/ICU** = Extreme/Intense Close Up, **MCU** = Medium Close Up
POV = Point Of View (the camera sees what someone or something sees)
FADE (IN/OUT) = go to or come from black
X-FADE = overlap going from one picture to the next
CUT TO = jump from one picture to the next
SLO MO = Slow Motion
PAN = camera shot moves across or back and forth
ANGLE = position of camera shot
SFX = Sound effects
SUPER = Super-impose: overlap pictures or picture and text (i.e. 'One week later")

Useful information on a Script Page ("Side")

PAGE # - Upper right hand corner - Lets you know generally where you are in the story
SCENE # - Usually in both margins wherever a new scene starts - Lets you know when there's a new scene, new camera set up or new location. NEW SCENE # DOES NOT ALWAYS MEAN THE END OF THE SCENE. It can just be a change of location or camera set up, but is a continuation of dialogue.
LOCATION & TIME - (i.e., EXT - COFFEE SHOP - DAY) – Tells you where and when the following dialogue takes place and may include camera angle info. Other directions may follow.
ACTION DIRECTIONS - Are typed from margin to margin (or somewhat wider than the dialogue margins) and explain visual activity or events.
CHARACTER DESCRIPTIONS - Are usually within the ACTION DIRECTIONS and are used only when a character appears for the first time in the script. They usually contain physical and/or background information. (i.e., BOB BROWN, a 35 yr. old, dark haired lawyer enters)
CHARACTER DIRECTIONS - Are usually in brackets ( ) and are next to the character's name within the dialogue, or on a separate line within the dialogue.
DIALOGUE - Usually typed within narrow margins down the middle of the page and may have ACTION or CHARACTER DIRECTIONS in between.

Example: Scene taken directly from a script*

```
*"The Last Christmas"
 With permission of Geoffrey Redknap, author
 All rights reserved, Goonworks Films
```

```
1 INT. HOUSE - DAY                                              1

BISCUIT the cat paws at a jingle bell dog ornament hanging
on a Christmas tree. On the couch, JOSH, 10, awakens with a
start. He looks to the front door, before spotting Biscuit.

                        JOSH
                Biscuit. Get out of that.
The cat runs off.
An idyllic Christmas scene. Vintage decorations and candles
dominate the home of an elderly couple. Thirty year old
furniture, frilly covers, shelves lined with a lifetime of
photos and mementos. Josh rubs weary eyes and looks to a
completed Christmas jigsaw puzzle. He pulls a section out
of the middle and sets the pieces aside. Josh removes several
ornaments from the tree, putting them back in their box.

2 INT. KITCHEN - DAY                                            2
Josh shakes the last of a can of oatmeal into a pot of boiling
water on a stove. From the bedroom, a clatter.

                     NANA (O.S.)
                 Who's in my kitchen?

                        JOSH
             It's okay, Nana. It's Josh.

                     NANA (O.S.)
                  You're what?

                        JOSH
                Josh. Remember. I slept over.
Josh covers the pot, takes a slow breath then approaches the
bedroom doorway.
```

Example: Scene created for the audition

(Scene written by Linda Darlow)

ONE: Where were you?

TWO: Out. I had some errands to run.

ONE: Like what?

TWO: Just some errands................

ONE: Why can't you tell me?

TWO: They were just errands!

ONE: You're lying, aren't you. You went to see him (her)!

TWO: Yeah, okay................ so what if I did!

As you can see, this scene has no scene numbers, or stage directions or character's names.

You might get this kind of material if the script isn't ready, or if no one is allowed to see any portion of the real script yet.

Usually, when you get the sides they've been marked by the casting director as to where you will "start" reading and where you will "stop".

Example: (scene from "Auburn Hills Breakdown", by Geoffrey Redknap, Goonworks Films, All rights reserved)

12.

```
                    DAN (CONT'D)
          Those are for you, and we'll see          *
          you for breakfast.                        *

     Dan closes the door. Junior, nervously, looks around the     *
     overly decorative room. He sees the pajamas and toiletries.  *
```

START 16   INT. LIVING ROOM - EVENING   16

```
     Ma is stretched out on the couch beneath a frilly comforter.
     Behind her head, a huge, matching pillow.

                    LOUISE
          If you're all set, I'm off to bed.         *

                    MA
          I couldn't be more comfortable. You
          all have been so nice.

                    LOUISE
          Happy to have you. Nightie, night.         *

     She heads up the stairs. Ma's usual dower expression is
     noticeably absent, replaced with a relaxed smile.
```

STOP

```
  17    INT. SPARE BEDROOM - EVENING                       17

     Junior attempts to sharpen his toothbrush into a shank, using   *
     a ceramic frog. He listens as Louise's footsteps echo up the    *
     stairs. He hears the door open and close. Junior continues.     *
     Muffled voices, the sound of furniture being slid across the    *
     floor. After a long pause, he hears a slow rhythmic thumping.

     Junior stops, as he realizes he is hearing the sound of the     *
     most functional Sunday night sex imaginable. Junior             *
     unwittingly breaks his shank.                                   *

  18    INT. CHILD'S BEDROOM - EVENING                     18

     Shinpei, still gaming, knows the Sunday night routine.
     Without pausing, he turns up the volume on his game.

     Girl takes the opportunity to attack his character. Sounds of
     video game death.

                    SHINPEI
          Hey, no fair.

     Pleased by her growing skills, Shinpei offers a sly smirk.
```

Occasionally, there are internal cuts in the scene that are marked as such. Think of these markings as your road map and follow that map.

Example: (scene from "Heaven's Door", by Geoffrey Redknap, Goonworks Films, all rights reserved)

```
66    CONTINUED:                                              66

           She only glares at him.  Callum dashes down the aisles.
           Peering over and pushing through the clutter.

                          CALLUM (CONT'D)
                     Marcus!

                          MARCUS (O.S.)
                     I like this one.

           Looking around a magazine rack, he's shocked to find Marcus
           sitting on the floor, quietly reading a comic.

                          LINDA
                     Beeb.  Appreciate if you didn't let
                     your boy run amok.

           Teresa reluctantly enters, hanging by the door.

                          LINDA (CONT'D)
                     Wouldn't have expected you.

           Teresa is uncomfortably silent.

           Callum kneels before Marcus, grabbing his shoulders.

                          CALLUM
                     What did I say about wandering off?

           Marcus is scared silent.

                          CALLUM (CONT'D)
                     I need you to smarten up!  Okay?

                          MARCUS
                     Okay.

           Callum hugs Marcus.
```

~ 9 ~

There may also be pages that are sent to you marked "F.Y.I." which means For Your Information only. *You will not be reading these.* They are given to help you understand your character better or give you more historical information about your character's involvement in the script. **Example: (Scene written by Henry Mah)**

3.

2   INT. AUDITION WAITING ROOM – 20 MINUTES LATER   2

The door opens to the audition room and out come the CASTING
AGENT and SARAH BRONSON, both laughing jovially.

                         CASTING AGENT
                    Thank you, Sarah. Good to see you
                    again.

BOB MORROW pops out the door briefly.

                         BOB
                    Thanks for coming in. Give me a
                    call, Sarah.

                         SARAH
                    Thanks for bringing me in again,
                    Bob. Take care.

BOB scans the waiting room briefly, then gives SARAH a wave
and returns to the audition room. As SARAH signs out she
leaves the room in a flourish. The tone of the room returns
to a nervous somberness.

                         CASTING AGENT
                    Let's have Julie Mason, please.
                    Julie Mason.

                         JULIE
                    Here. I'm right here.

                         CASTING AGENT
                    Yes. Thank you for coming in. This
                    way, please.

JULIE rises and enters the room. The door closes behind her.

3   INT. AUDITION ROOM – CONTINUOUS   3

The door closes behind JULIE as she is pointed to the centre
of the room. The CASTING AGENT moves behind a table, where we
see three stern looking people BOB, JAN and TOM watching
JULIE closely.

                         CASTING AGENT
                    Bob Morrow, producer, Jan Banks,
                    producer, and Tom Kelsay the
                    director. Everyone, Julie Mason.

                         JULIE
                    Nice to meet you.

JULIE goes over and extends her hand to BOB MORROW, who
hesitantly extends his out to her.

(handwritten annotations: F.Y.I., START, ↓ CONT.)

CAUTION!

Frequently, in dialogue on a page, there will be stage directions describing what's happening visually: what characters are doing, how they're feeling, or what they're seeing. These directions are separated from the dialogue or they will be in parenthesis ( ) in between sentences.

Sometimes this separation for stage directions comes in the middle of a character's speech. When this happens, they re-title the character's name as if it's a new speech but in fact it may be a continuation of the speech before.

Most actors seem to think this is meant to be a pause, or they just keep forgetting that the next line is still theirs. Look for these instances. Mark the script in a way that reminds you to keep talking.

Example: (scene from "Heaven's Door", by Geoffrey Redknap, Goonworks Prod, all rights reserved)

```
3    CONTINUED:                                                        3
                          ELLIS (CONT'D)
                 You know, this really is a decent
                 place.  I mean, like I said, apart
                 from the location.  Me, I can't take
                 these winters.  Each harder than the
                 last.  Nope.  I'm out.

     Ellis looks around the store.

                          ELLIS (CONT'D)
                 You must know everyone appreciates
                 this place.  After work ritual.
                 Coming in here for a pack of smokes,
                 some beer.  Frozen dinner and a movie.
                      (pause)
                 Wiper fluid.

     Ellis reaches for a jug, but something else catches his eye.

                          ELLIS (CONT'D)
                 Those what I think they are?

     The cashier remains silent.
```

<u>NOTE</u>:

Scenes don't always start at the top of a page. You may need to look for the logical start of the scene if it isn't marked. Sometimes the scene will be marked incorrectly and actually start before or after the spot the casting director has marked. Read everything on the page carefully. Make sure you know where it *makes sense* to start and stop.

Example: (scene written by Henry Mah)

                                                                                    10.

                                    ANIA
                        What kind of product?

                                                            CUT TO:

    11   EXT. GROCERY STORE - SAME DAY, CONTINUOUS   11

                ANIA and JULIE emerge from the grocery store, where we see
                lined up an array of vegetables. Protruding from JULIE'S bag
                is a long English cucumber.

    START   JULIE
                        Hair spray.

                                    ANIA
                        Hair spray?

                                    JULIE
                        How was I to know that he was just
                        tossing empty cans in the garbage?

                                    ANIA
                        You sure took him out good.

                                    JULIE
                        Too good. They want me to demo
                        tomorrow.

                                    ANIA
                        How to take someone down and not
                        mess up your hair?

                                    JULIE
                        Pretty much.

Before you start *acting,* there is more information to gather from the pages you have that will help you with making choices.

Look for the following on your sides:

1 – **Page number:** tells you where in the script this scene appears

2 – **Scene number, location of scene, time of day:** gives you your "place"

3 – **Stage directions:** fills in visuals, gives you your physical/emotional life.

<u>NOTE:</u> Regarding all stage directions: Read them all, but *do not* feel obligated to perform them -- especially emotional ones!

(Scene from "Heaven's Door" by Geoffrey Redknap, Goonworks Films, all rights reserved)

```
        WHITE Revision  -  7-10-12                        65.


   87   EXT. DIXON FARMHOUSE - NIGHT                             87

        The front door is wide open.  Inside is dark and quiet.
        Death owns this place, except for the two vehicles idling
        out front.  One is Thomas' sedan.  The other, a ominous black
        truck.

        Thomas flounders through the snow, as he approaches a lean
        man standing beside the truck.  ANGUS BISMARK, mid-thirties,
        a cold precise weapon and the reason Ellis Dixon doesn't
        carry a gun.  He diligently watches the lifeless house.

                        THOMAS
                You're not going in?

                        ANGUS
                The man said, stay.

                        THOMAS
                It's fucking cold.

                        ANGUS
                Just do your job.  He'll come out
                when he's finished.

        They look to the empty doorway.  Wind carried snow disappears
        into the darkness.
```

CHAPTER 2

The Twelve Choices:

Now that you've read the breakdown and have your sides prepared, you're ready to start working on analyzing the scene/scenes. *It's not time to start acting yet.* You must spend some time reading through the material as if you were reading a novel, just to get a sense of what the scene is about. I recommend you read the scene at least 10 times, if not more, before you start saying one word out loud. I guarantee that each time you read through it you will discover something you missed.

When you are finished reading for information, don't start acting yet. The next step will be to make some choices and answer some questions regarding your character's situation in the scene.

The following Twelve Choices, Mr. Shurtleff calls Guideposts, are the ones that will help you the most in your preparation. I have taken the liberty of re-ordering his list and re-naming some of them to better suit preparing for a film audition. Basically, my Twelve Choices and his Guideposts are the same. I mention this in case you have read or will read (and I recommend you do) his book, *Audition*. I don't want you to be confused.

The first six on my list apply to every audition scene no matter what. They even apply to one-line, one word and no-line scenes as well. The second six on my list *may or may not* apply to every scene. They are extensions of the first six and come up frequently in scripted material.

Make a decision about how to play a scene based on these choices. It will be all you need to do in order to execute the scene with confidence and clarity.

THE TWELVE CHOICES

<u>FIRST SIX</u>

These choices should be made for every scene you will prepare. They are basic decisions for any scene regardless of its length, and are the building blocks of even the shortest one-liner. All situations, no matter how brief or extensive, contain these elements and *must* be considered:

1. PLACE

2. MOMENT BEFORE/MOMENT AFTER

3. RELATIONSHIP

4. FIGHTING FOR

5. IMPORTANCE

6. LISTENING/DISCOVERY

<u>SECOND SIX</u>

These choices *may or may not* apply to a scene. They are, for the most part, extensions of the first six and help to add depth and color to the material. Any one or more of these choices may define what the scene is about; or they may not fit the scene at all. Don't try to force them when they do not apply. Many scenes do contain these elements and should be considered when analyzing material. They are:

7. POSITION

8. EVENTS

9. ROLE PLAYING/GAME PLAYING

10. MYSTERY/SECRET

11. HUMOR

12. OPPOSITES

Michael Shurtleff's definition of an audition:

"...the real you reacting to a remarkable situation in a unique way..."

"...the real you..." Who you really are. Be yourself. Cast yourself in the role.

    <u>Choices that support this:</u> *relationship, position, game/role -playing*

"...reacting to..." Acting is reacting. Hear or see something to react to.
                    Listening is everything.
    <u>Choices that support this:</u> *place, moment before, fighting for, listening/discovery*

"...a remarkable situation..." They don't write scenes about nothing happening.

    <u>Choices that support this:</u> *events, importance, mystery/secret*

"In a unique way..." Your way is the unique way. Don't try to be different.
                If you're being yourself, you are different.

    <u>Choices that support this:</u> *humor, opposites*

Understanding his definition is all you need in order to deliver a good audition. When you want to know if you're making the right choice, just weigh it against this definition; if it fits, it's the right choice. Now on to what those twelve choices mean.

THE TWELVE CHOICES

1. PLACE

"Where are you" *literally* in the scene?

> ➤ <u>Be specific</u>* and make it familiar.
> ➤ <u>See</u> the environment around you.

How can you *use* it physically?

How can you *let us know* where you are?

How do you *feel* about being there?

*By "specific", I mean not just in what room but *where in that room?*
For example, I'm in the living room… but *where?* Are you sitting on the sofa, standing by the window, sitting at a desk, or at the front door?

<u>Suggestions for auditions:</u>

- ❖ Read stage directions for place and use that place if it supports what you can do easily in the room.
- ❖ Alter stage directions if literal place is too logistically difficult to execute.
- ❖ Keep it simple, do-able, clear and appropriate to the scene.

<u>Results of making this choice:</u>

- ✓ You always know whether you're sitting or standing.
- ✓ It creates a visual picture for your audience.
- ✓ Grounds you in the reality of the scene.
- ✓ Makes you feel more comfortable and secure.
- ✓ Helps you focus on the situation.

2. <u>MOMENT BEFORE:</u>

What are you *doing** in the moment **before**
the dialogue starts?

> ➢ Find a physical activity to do.
> ➢ Know how you are feeling.

What's on your mind?

What have you just heard?

What has just happened?

*By "doing" I mean any simple activity requiring physical movement.
For example, "I'm standing here talking to someone" isn't enough. What are you doing while you talk... are you fixing your hair, playing with your ring, etc.

<u>Suggestions for auditions:</u>

- ❖ Get ideas from the script or create your own if there are no hints in the script.
- ❖ Make sure your choice is in keeping with the scene. Don't be too wildly creative with your ideas.
- ❖ Make your choice immediate, simple, and specific.
- ❖ Start the scene with your moment before.
- ❖ Express it in feeling and doing something.

<u>Results of making this choice:</u>

- ✓ Can quickly get you where you need to be emotionally for the rest of the scene; then you can just let it happen.

2. **MOMENT BEFORE** (cont'd)

Results of making this choice: (cont'd)

- ✓ Gives the audience something to watch, not just something to listen to.
- ✓ Helps you focus and get deeper into the scene.
- ✓ Gives you a moment more of camera time especially if you only have a line or two.

NOTE: Your choice of a moment before can be critical. If you choose *wisely*, it will make the execution of the rest of the scene much easier. If you choose *unwisely*, you will spend the entire scene fighting an uphill battle to get where you need to be.

For example: A scene may be about having a fight with someone. You will need to be agitated and get angry during it. Therefore:

A *wise* moment before might be to have trouble with finding something, or to be frustrated with something you're doing (shuffling papers, fixing a latch, etc.).

An *unwise* moment before would be to have your feet up on the desk, sipping coffee. You'll have much farther to go to get angry from this relaxed position.

2a. <u>MOMENT AFTER:</u>

What are you *doing* in the moment ***after***
the dialogue ends?

> ➤ Find a physical activity.
> ➤ Have a reaction to what's gone on.

<u>Suggestions for auditions:</u>

- ❖ Keep your life going after the dialogue has ended just for a beat or two.
- ❖ Go back to what you were doing at the beginning of the scene, or carry on to the next logical activity.
- ❖ You may add a word or two, or just react physically.
- ❖ If the other character has the last line, your moment comes *after* that line.

<u>Results of making this choice:</u>

- ✓ Gives the scene completion.
- ✓ Keeps you from dropping out of the scene before it's really over.
- ✓ Keeps you from looking on tape like a *deer caught in the headlights*.
- ✓ Keeps you from commenting on your work while the camera is still rolling.

<u>NOTE:</u> The moment after isn't as important as the moment before, but it finishes off the scene nicely and completes your presentation for the audience. You now have a scene with a beginning, middle and end.

3. RELATIONSHIP

How do you *feel* about the person you are talking to?

> ➢ Who are they to you?
> ➢ How do you feel about them *right now**?

*If you know more about the relationship (friend, lover, client, etc.), fine, but watch out for trying to play *past history* of the relationship in this *present* time.

Suggestions for auditions:

- ❖ If you aren't sure of what the relationship is between characters have your agent get clarification for you.
- ❖ If your agent is unable to (or you don't have an agent), ask the auditors.
- ❖ Make sure your choice is in keeping with what the scene suggests.
- ❖ Always make the choice, even if this is the first time you're meeting the other character.
- ❖ Consider where the love (or absence of love) is and how it can be communicated in the scene.

NOTE: You must choose only one: you either *like* or *don't like* the other character. If you hear yourself saying, "I like them <u>but</u> I don't like them", you are in trouble. Watch out for the "but" word! If you use it, you are about to weaken a strong choice. You can only communicate *one* of those feelings at a time.
You *can* change your mind; you may start out liking the person and during the scene then change your opinion to not liking them -- or vice versa.

3. **RELATIONSHIP:** (cont'd)

Results of making this choice:

- ✓ It gets your attention off yourself and on to the other person in the scene.
- ✓ It gives the scene a sense of attitude that shows without your needing to determine how to say a line.
- ✓ It may be what the whole scene is about, in which case you had better make some clear choices.

4. FIGHTING FOR

What are you fighting for in the scene and how are you going to get it?

> *For,* not *against* – make your goal a positive one.
> It's the same thing as "objective".
> What can you do tha*t is within your control* to get what you want?

NOTE: This choice seems to be one of the *trickier* ones for actors; it is also one of the more important ones.

There are two levels to consider:
1 – The <u>materialistic</u> thing you want or event you want to have happen.
Examples: to get money, to get information, to get out, to get in, etc.

2 – The <u>psychological</u> satisfaction you will feel from getting what you want.
Examples: to be happy, to feel secure, etc.

You must also consider how you're going to get it:

What is in your control?
If you want someone to like you, you can't control whether they do or not; but you can control what you *do* to get them to like you.
Examples: I can look good, be charming, be nice to them, etc.

It's also about winning and losing.
You need to notice how it's going. Are you getting what you want or not? If you are, then keep doing what you're doing; if not, then you need to change your tactics.
Example: first I'll try being nice, but that doesn't work, so then I'll turn on the charm, etc.

4. **FIGHTING FOR:** (cont'd)

Another example: If you want someone to do something for you, you can start by bargaining with them. But that doesn't work, so you plead with them and that doesn't work. Finally you threaten them and that works. The dialogue will most likely suggest what tactics to try; if not, choose your own.

Suggestions for auditions:
- ❖ State your choice in a few words. Make it clear and specific in one sentence.
- ❖ The psychological choice may have to come more from what works for you personally unless it is clearly defined in the character's lines.
- ❖ Make your choice based on what is going on in the scene.*

*What the dialogue is saying may *not* be exactly what you are fighting for. You may have to dig a little deeper or look at the broader context to discover what your choice should be in this situation. Your choice may need to be simpler or more abstract than what the dialogue suggests.

Results of making this choice:
- ✓ You have a task to focus on and get involved in beyond "I hope I get this job".
- ✓ It gives you a course of action to follow — something *to do and a way of being* in the scene.
- ✓ It brings life and energy to the scene. The more you're involved, the more the audience is involved.

5. IMPORTANCE

How important is it that you get what you want?
> ➤ Make it a matter of life & death.
> ➤ Maximize the situation personally.
>   "What's in it for me?"
> ➤ Make the stakes really high, even if
>   what the character wants seems trivial.*

*They don't write scenes about nothing happening. It may not seem all that important to you, but it's very important to the *character*.

Example: A scene is never about two people just talking -- there's always something more going on. You need to find out what it is your character wants out of having the conversation and make it a matter of life and death that he/she gets it.

Example: If the scene is about your character ordering lunch in a restaurant, it may not seem important. But how important would it be if you were very hungry, or you didn't have much time and a waitress was ignoring you? At that moment I'm sure it would be a matter of life or death.

Suggestions for auditions:
> ❖ You must know what you're *fighting for*
>   in order to make it important.
> ❖ Make it personally important, both
>   psychologically and emotionally.

Results of making this choice:
> ✓ It will give the scene the right
>   level of intensity.
> ✓ Helps your focus and concentration.
> ✓ Gives the scene energy and personal
>   involvement.

6. LISTENING/DISCOVERY

What do you see or hear that you are reacting to?

- ➢ *Acting* is *reacting*.
- ➢ You must hear or see something to react to.
- ➢ You must hear or see it *for the first time*.

NOTE: Listening is the key to good acting. Here are a few extra points:

-- Hear what the other character says and *how* it is said. What's *between* the lines?

-- You must be aware of new information your character is hearing and allow your character to react to the new discovery.

-- You, the actor, have read the scene and know what the other character says, but the character you're playing doesn't know; so you need to forget that you know and react as though it's the first time you're hearing it too.

-- In order to be listening, you *must not* be thinking of your next line, or what you are doing, or how the scene is going. You *must* have your full attention on the other character (the reader). If you have prepared properly you can let go of those thoughts, be in the moment, and let your reactions happen.

-- If you are really listening at that moment, your reactions may be different than when you rehearsed it; but trust that if you understand the character's situation, your reaction will be appropriate. My *Staying Away From the Material* exercise in Chapter 3 of this section will help you practice listening. Use it!

Suggestions for the audition:

- ❖ Really listen to the other person reading with you. If they aren't giving you what you expected, hear what you need from the words.

6. <u>LISTENING/DISCOVERY:</u> (cont'd)

❖ It's so important to hear what's being said that if you realize you weren't listening, or you literally can't hear the reader, you must do what you would do in life when you haven't heard someone – *get them to repeat what they said.* Say: "What?", "Could you repeat that?", or "Sorry, I didn't hear what you said".

❖ *Never look at your script while the other person is talking*; listen to them first. If you still don't know your next line, look at your page when they have finished talking. If you hear what they say it might just remind you of your next line and you won't need to look. It feels like it takes forever but it doesn't.

<u>Results of making this choice:</u>

✓ It helps get your attention off yourself and on to the other person and the situation in the scene.

✓ If you've done your homework on the scene, *listening* is the only thing you need to do when you're in the audition (after you have established your *place* and *moment before*).

✓ It gives you something to *react* to.

✓ It keeps you from anticipating what the reader is saying and keeps you from reacting before they've finished saying it.

✓ It keeps you from playing the end of the scene before you get there.

<u>SPECIAL NOTE:</u> *Listening* in an audition is probably the biggest and most valuable favor you can do for yourself. If you're not listening the audience can tell!

REMINDER: These next six choices may or may not be applicable to the scene you're doing. Don't try to force them into a scene when they don't apply.

7. POSITION

Are you taking a strong enough stand for what you are fighting for in the scene?

➢ Be self-righteous and passionate.
➢ "I'm right." "You're wrong, and you should change."
➢ Be willing to intrude.
➢ Personally get behind your character's position.*

*It's important to find a way to make your character's position your own. If you don't, you're likely to play your *judgment* of someone who takes that position. If you are a non-confrontational person in real life, it will be hard to express your righteousness. Unless you can feel as strongly as the character feels about the subject, you may need to substitute something you are righteous about.

Suggestions for auditions:

❖ Don't be afraid to be disliked. You're only pretending and it's your chance to express yourself.
❖ You can be as nice as you want to be, you just have to take a strong stand. You don't have to be mean or nasty to be strong.
❖ The audience needs to know that you are unshakeable in your resolve.

Results of making this choice:

✓ Creates immediate and personal conflict.
✓ Involves you more deeply in the situation.
✓ Gives the scene more intensity.
✓ Helps create the struggle the other character needs to work against.

8. EVENTS

Where are the *discoveries* you make in the
scene that *change your course of action?*

- ➤ Closely related to *listening/discovery.*
- ➤ What do you see or hear that makes you
  reconsider what to do next?
- ➤ When are you winning or losing at getting
  what you want?
- ➤ Given the new information, how do you feel
  and what do you do now?
- ➤ Events may be minor or life-changing.

Suggestions for auditions:

- ❖ Look through the scene, find the events and
  mark them, so you remember where they are.
- ❖ Make the decision whether it is a major or minor
  event; whether you are winning or losing, and then
  think about how you would react.
- ❖ In the audition you must *see or hear* what causes
  the event *at that moment* and let yourself react.
- ❖ Give yourself a moment to process the reaction/decision
  before you speak.

Results of making this choice:

- ✓ Gives a sense of life happening in the scene
  beyond just saying the lines.
- ✓ Allows you to really live in the moment.
- ✓ Reminds you to experience what's happening.
- ✓ Sometimes the silent moments are the most
  interesting parts of a scene.
- ✓ The audience feels more included in your process.
- ✓ Makes your character (and you) more interesting.

9. ROLE PLAYING/GAME PLAYING

Based on your actual relationship, are you playing a *literal* or *behavioral* game with the other character?

- ➤ Literally, who are you to that person?
- ➤ Behaviorally, how do you treat that person?
- ➤ What are the rules of the game?
- ➤ Who is in the power position; or are you equal in status?

Here are some examples:

LITERAL ROLE	BEHAVIORAL ROLE PLAYING
Mother/Daughter	Mother/Daughter (same as literal)
Mother/Daughter	Daughter/Mother (behavioral)
Sister/Sister	Sister/Sister (literal))
Sister/Sister	Mother/Daughter (behavioral)
Loan Officer/Applicant	Prison Guard/Inmate (behavioral)

NOTE:

We treat people differently depending on our relationship with them. The situation in the scene will usually dictate how these characters interact, regardless of their literal relationship. Sometimes they behave according to their literal relationship as expected; so that's how you should treat the other character. Sometimes they play a different game with each other. Identify the roles in this game and treat the other character accordingly.

You can also use this choice in the audition when you're given a direction to "be warmer", "be tougher", etc. Instead of trying to play the direction, change the role playing you're using; the behavior will automatically change. Example: the direction is to be warmer; so use "Teacher/Young Student" instead of "Mother/Daughter".

9. ROLE PLAYING/GAME PLAYING: (cont'd)

Suggestions for auditions:

❖ Play the role and the game for real.
❖ Don't act like you're playing a game.
❖ Be specific in identifying the literal/behavioral roles.
❖ You must identify *both* characters' roles.
❖ Keep the stakes high and play the game well.

NOTE: We play many different roles in our real life relationships. Sometimes we play different roles with the same people. For instance, I play the role of Teacher to Student in class, but if we're at a party the roles change to Peer/Peer and we're on an equal level. The rules of the game change according to the roles we play and the circumstances of the situation.

I think Shakespeare's speech, *"All the world's a stage, and all the men and women merely players..."* exemplifies this choice.

Results of making this choice:

✓ Adds color to your attitude without your having to play it.
✓ Sets a tone for the scene naturally without having to think about line readings.
✓ Gives your character definition in the relationship.
✓ Makes a direction you're given easier to execute.

WORTH REPEATING: When you use this choice, you must identify both your role and the other character's role. You can't have one without the other.

For example: If you play the role of a Father, then you must identify the role of the person you're talking to. Is it Father to Son? Or is it Father to Mother? The *rules* of the game based on those roles are very different.

10. MYSTERY/SECRET

Does your character have a secret, or is your character in mystery?

- ➤ What's your secret?
- ➤ What's the other character's secret?
- ➤ Is your character missing information?
- ➤ Is the other character missing information?
- ➤ Are you both missing information?
- ➤ Is there a sense of the *unknown*, *wonderment* and/or *curiosity*?

If your character has a secret is the secret:

- Something you would *never* tell?
  (then hide it well)
- Something that, if pressed, you *would* tell?
  (then be aware you have a secret)
- Something you are *dying* to tell?
  (then drop hints all over the place)

If your character is in mystery do you:

- Suspect you're missing something?
  (then be curious)
- Not suspect anything?
  (then be clueless)

NOTE: If your character has a secret, you may have to make it a little obvious so the audience gets it; pretend the other character is unaware of how obvious you're making it.

10. **MYSTERY/SECRET:** (cont'd)

Suggestions for auditions:

❖ If your secret is something you would never tell, don't play Mystery/Secret.

❖ If you are in mystery and don't suspect anything, don't play Mystery/Secret.

❖ Don't make up secrets regarding the plot line unless it clearly exists in the scene.

❖ If it adds to your character's personality and personal interaction, then make it up – *if it doesn't affect the plot or change the story line*.

❖ You may also consider what you don't know about yourself.

Results of making this choice:

✓ It might be needed to inform the audience.

✓ Adds another level to what you are fighting for if it's appropriate.

✓ Helps keep you *in the moment* in the scene.

✓ Always adds to the drama and intrigue, which comes up frequently in scripts.

11. HUMOR

Does your character have a sense of humor?

- Humor is not about telling jokes or being funny.
- It's what makes life bearable, bad as it may be.
- There is always humor even in the most serious drama.
- It gives one a sense of hope that things will get better.

NOTE: It is also possible that your character does not have a sense of humor, or has temporarily lost it. Humor is not about making something funny or doing comedy. In fact, if you want something to be comedic, *don't* have a sense of humor – it's usually funnier.

Suggestions for auditions:

- ❖ Decide if your character has a sense of humor or not.
- ❖ Use your sense of humor in the role. Make sure you have one first.
- ❖ If you have trouble identifying with a character, it may be because they don't have a sense of humor; or you don't and they do.

NOTE OF CAUTION: If you personally have a strong sense of humor, it's more difficult to play a character that doesn't. It will require an enormous amount of focus and concentration to totally suppress yours; so be aware that given the slightest provocation your sense of humor might flash through.

11. __HUMOR:__ (cont'd)

Results of making this choice:

✓ Helps bring your unique energy and vibration to the scene.
✓ Fills out your character's personality.
✓ Gives the audience a sense of hope for the character.
✓ May bring a moment of lightness to an otherwise dark situation.

<u>Now is a good time to mention this:</u> With regard to your emotional life in a scene, characters are usually fighting to maintain control, not to lose it; they are fighting to survive, not to give in. No matter how bad it gets, human beings have a strong survival instinct. If they let their emotions rule, people are less likely to get what they want -- unless they're using their emotions on purpose to get it.

Humor may help temper an emotional flare up. You can choose to use the character's sense of humor to inhibit an outburst.

12. <u>OPPOSITES</u>

Where are the *inconsistencies* in the scene and in your character?

> ➤ Human behavior is inconsistent.
> ➤ Only actors behave consistently.
> ➤ *Consistency is the heart of dull acting.* (Shurtleff)
> ➤ Human beings are unaware of their inconsistencies; actors need to be *aware* of them.
> ➤ Identifying opposites will clarify inconsistencies.

<u>What is an opposite?</u>
The best way to describe an opposite is to give you some examples:

- Where there is love, hate also exists.
- Where there is decision there is also doubt.
- Where there is energy there is tiredness.
- If day exists, there must be something not day, ergo night.

<u>Other areas that contain *opposites*</u>:
<u>PHYSICAL</u>: saying one thing but physically demonstrating the opposite:

- Saying, "yes"/shaking head no
- Saying, "three"/holding up two fingers
- Saying, "down"/pointing up

<u>MENTAL</u>: saying one thing but thinking the opposite (lying):

- "I didn't take it"/thinking, "I did take it"
- "You look beautiful"/thinking, "You look terrible"

<u>EMOTIONAL</u>: saying how you feel but expressing the opposite:

- "I'm so happy!"/while crying
- "I'm angry!"/while laughing

12. OPPOSITES: (cont'd)

Suggestions for auditions:

- ❖ There are opposites in every scene. Look for them.
- ❖ You may have to dig a little, but it's worth it.
- ❖ Be selective, there's no need to make everything an opposite.
- ❖ Identify the specific literal choice first, then find the *extreme* opposite.
- ❖ If you choose the extreme opposite of an expression, it creates all possibilities in-between and will likely occur instinctively.
- ❖ Don't use them if you don't feel comfortable or confident in executing them.
- ❖ If you do use them, be bold and commit to the choice.
- ❖ Transition quickly* and smoothly.

Humans transition in an instant from one way of being to another. *Actors* tend to take too much time *transitioning* from moment to moment.

Results of making this choice:

- ✓ It helps develop conflict within your character and in the scene.
- ✓ Creates complex character development.
- ✓ Brings concentration and focus to a high level.
- ✓ Is fascinating for the audience to watch.

NOTE: Executing opposites is a way of exploring character idiosyncrasies without changing who you are. If you apply enough of them, you should start to notice characteristics emerge that are *different* from your own.

CHAPTER 3

EMOTIONAL CONNECTION:

You may have noticed that there is no choice called "Emotion". That's because you don't need to make a pre-determined choice in that area; and besides, you can't really know how the character is feeling until you've figured out what's going on in the scene. Unfortunately, it's usually the *first* choice an actor wants to make; sometimes it's the *only* choice. Many actors put all of their attention on the emotional life without doing any other analysis of the material. They think that being emotional is what acting is. *It is not.*

The character's emotional life should be generated by the circumstances of the situation. You need to understand those circumstances before you can explore how the character feels. Since *you* are the character, you should look at how this situation makes *you* feel.

If you make the choices I am covering, your emotional life should come up naturally. If you know what you're fighting for in the scene, you'll know how far you should allow yourself to go emotionally.

Emotions can get in the way of getting what you want. If you are feeling a strong emotion, it's in your nature to hold the emotion back more than to let it rage. In scenes, as in life, it's more important to get what you want than to express yourself emotionally. Of course, there may be times when the emotion just can't be held back, but it might be at the cost of getting what you want.

Actors tend to make the mistake of being more interested in the character *emoting* than in the character *surviving*; but isn't life more about survival, and isn't that more interesting?

1. NOT EVERY SCENE IS EMOTIONALLY INTENSE

Watch out for this one! Actors tend to think that every scene needs to be highly emotionally charged, but that's not always the case. Some scenes are about handling normal everyday activities that are important but not intensely emotional. You don't need to show them your full emotional range if you're the clerk serving a customer. You just need to serve the customer.

Actors don't feel like they're acting unless they're emoting, but actors should never feel like they're acting anyway. Your priority as the character should be to accomplish something first. If feelings come up, so be it. In real life people usually try to *suppress* more than *express* emotions. When you're preparing, analyze the scene first and your emotional life will fall into place.

2. FOLLOWING STAGE DIRECTIONS

I'm not a fan of following any stage directions – but I'm especially not a fan of following *emotional* stage directions, for example; *she cries, he shouts angrily*, etc.

You should read all stage directions to get a sense of what the writers are visualizing, but do not feel obligated to follow them. Many actors think they must follow those directions, but then they run the risk of having to fake the feeling in the audition.

Writers can't help themselves from visualizing the scene, including the emotional life of their characters; but think of it this way – the writer didn't know you when he/she wrote the script. You may have a different interpretation of the character's emotional life: one that suits you better, is real for you, and actually suits the scene better. Go with yours.

Most directors don't pay much attention to those stage directions and would rather see your interpretation, your emotional reaction. They just want the feeling, whatever it is, to be convincingly real.

In the audition it's best to go with how you are really feeling in the moment. Why decide ahead of time how you're going to feel, or force yourself to follow the stage directions? As I said, if you do that, you're in danger of faking it and believe me it shows; there's nothing worse than watching someone trying to cry when they're clearly not feeling it.

If the director wants a different emotional tone, he/she will give you a direction and have you do it again. If the director asks (which rarely happens), why you played it the way you did you should reply "That's how I was really feeling", then offer to try it differently. When you go with how you really feel, directors will never call you a bad actor; they know you're supposed to really feel it.

3. LEAVE OPTIONS OPEN

There is no *right* way to feel in a scene; there is only how you *really* feel in the moment. When you're preparing an audition, it's best to consider a few options regarding how you (the character) might feel at any moment and leave that emotional door open.

If you've made all your choices and are committed to them, it should put you on an emotional path. But there may be more than one feeling that would be appropriate for you, so consider all options. You don't have to worry about the *right* feeling in the audition. How you feel *in the moment* will be the right feeling.

For instance, you've just gotten news of a death. You might be overcome with sadness, or you might be numb, or get angry; there's always more than one way to feel. If you leave yourself open to options and don't get stuck on one way to be, you've got a better chance of allowing how you feel in the moment to actually happen. If the emotion is real it will be right.

Now back to the news of a death...

Every time you read through the scene, it's brought up sadness. When you're in the audition and you hear the news, you don't feel that sadness. What should you do? Well, if you've considered other options, you have choices: maybe you should go with numbness, or at the moment you're angry that the sadness didn't come, so you should go with anger *since that's how you're really feeling*.

It's critical in film work, even in auditions, that you allow yourself spontaneous behavior. You need to allow *yourself* to be surprised in the performance. I've developed two exercises to help you be more comfortable in this area. I can explain them, but it's up to you to practice them.

4. <u>EXERCISE: FOLLOW THE FEELING</u>

This is an emotional workout. It's meant to be done in front of a group so you can be comfortable expressing emotions while others are watching. You can still benefit from doing it when you are alone to exercise being conscious of how you are feeling at any moment. You can also use it to *change* how you are feeling. It's a simple exercise, but not necessarily an easy one. It depends on how in touch you are with your feelings and how willing you are to express those feelings. The harder the exercise is for you; the more resistance you have to doing it, the more you probably need it.

<u>Here's how I set it up in class:</u>

❖ Stand in front of the group; relaxed with your hands at your sides.
❖ Make eye contact with people in the group.
❖ Notice any physical or emotional feelings that come up.
❖ Say, **"I feel... (and a word or sound that describes the feeling)"**
❖ Use your body and voice to communicate what the feeling looks and sounds like. **Exaggerate the communication and go bigger with the feeling as you repeat it.**
❖ **Don't stop to look for another feeling.** Keep communicating the same one until another feeling finds you. Allow yourself to go over the top, and don't think about it; another feeling will come up.
❖ Go with the new feeling, keep connecting and expressing the new feeling.
❖ Stay with that feeling and **keep expressing it** until another feeling comes up.
❖ Keep going for at least two minutes or until the teacher stops you.

4. __EXERCISE: FOLLOW THE FEELING__ (cont'd)

Here are a few things to look out for when doing the exercise:

> There's no right or wrong way to feel. Try not to express your *judgment* of what you feel, just express the feeling.

> The more you commit to the expression and the bigger you allow it to be, the sooner it will change. If you resist or hold back on the feeling you will get stuck.

> You may only have one feeling for the entire time. If that's how you really feel then that's okay.

> It may take a few tries at the exercise to allow true feelings to surface. The more you do it, the easier it gets.

> Don't anticipate how you're going to feel. You won't know until you are actually feeling it.

> Don't try to force a change of feelings. Let the feelings change you.

> Don't stop to think. Let the feelings roll and don't hold back.

> If you are thinking, be conscious of that. Say "I feel thinky", and think as hard as you can.

> It's okay to make up words like "thinky", "laughy", "giggly", etc.

> If you don't know what to call the feeling, ***make a sound*** that expresses it.

4. <u>EXERCISE: FOLLOW THE FEELING</u> (cont'd)

<u>Thoughts vs. Feelings</u>

Having done this exercise thousands of times, I've discovered that some students don't know the difference between *thought* and *feeling*. No wonder it's hard for some to express themselves emotionally! Here are some definitions according to Merriam Webster:

think, 1. ...to form or have in the mind

thought, 1a. ...the action or process of thinking, b. serious consideration

feel, 1b. ...to perceive by a physical sensation coming from discrete end organs

feeling, 1b. ...generalized bodily consciousness or sensation

In order to do this exercise you will need to know the difference. It is difficult at times to tell them apart, so here are a few tips:

-- If you hear yourself say, "I feel **like**..." you are about to communicate a thought not a feeling. You are going to make an abstract analogy to *describe* a feeling instead of directly identifying and *having* the feeling.

-- You know you're having a feeling if there are physical sensations; emotions always have physical sensations connected to them. For example, cold, hot, tired, sad, happy are all feelings – there are physical sensations present.

-- A feeling is *not* what someone else is doing to you. For example, "I feel watched", "I feel ignored" are not feelings. You have to take it a step further and ask yourself:

"How does it make me *feel* that I'm being watched?" (I feel uncomfortable.)

"How does it make me *feel* that I'm being ignored?" (I feel angry.)

4. EXERCISE: FOLLOW THE FEELING (cont'd)

Benefits of this exercise:

Why do this? Why torture yourself, make yourself uncomfortable and possibly upset for no reason? The obvious answer is that as an actor, your emotional life is part of your skill set. You need to be conversant with your own emotional life in order to use it in your work. You need to be able to express yourself fully in front of other people. You need to know how to access and manipulate your emotions. You need to be comfortable being *un*comfortable and vulnerable.

So this exercise:

- ✓ Trains you to be conscious of how you are feeling at any given moment.
- ✓ Makes you more comfortable expressing your feelings.
- ✓ Helps you see where you may resist expressing certain feelings.
- ✓ Allows you to explore your own emotional range and helps you find triggers for certain emotions.
- ✓ Exercises your ability to let go of mentally controlling feelings and frees your emotional expression.
- ✓ Encourages you to introduce more spontaneity in your work.

I compare this exercise to looking at the directory in the mall. You can easily find the store you want to get to on the map, but what else do you need to know in order to get there? You need to know *where you are at the moment*. The same is true with emotions. In order to get to a particular feeling, you need to be conscious of how you are feeling right now.

This exercise will also help in preparing for the next exercise which I call, "Staying Away from the Material".

5. EXERCISE: STAYING AWAY FROM THE MATERIAL

Actors tend to allow the lines to dictate how they should be feeling. They think it serves the scene to match their feeling to what the words are saying. It would seem like the logical and rational thing to do. However, emotional human behavior is anything *but* logical and rational. What we are literally saying and how we are actually feeling at that moment can be very different things.

We need to explore the illogical and irrational possibilities of a character's behavior. After we've made our choices and are ready to learn the lines, we should allow ourselves to go *outside of the logic box* and explore some *spontaneous* emotional behavior.

This exercise is designed to help you access your own spontaneous, illogical, irrational feelings and explore how they may or may not apply to the scene. It is also a tool for learning lines without learning a performance, which helps enormously in film work. You want to stay as flexible as possible with your lines so that you can accommodate any directions you may be given; make changes to your performance; allow the other actors to affect you; and *still remember the words*.

It's an unconscious process, but when we learn lines we tend to learn *line readings* as well. We repeat the same tone, rhythm and emphasis on certain words every time we go over them. In fact we come to rely on tone, rhythm and emphasis to help us remember the lines; so if we change any of those things we forget the line.

If you can learn the lines doing them differently every time you say them, you've got a better chance of knowing them well and staying flexible with your performance. Remember, there is no *right* way to say a line; there is only how you feel about it in the moment. If it's an honest and real reaction to what you hear, it will be right.

I do this exercise with my students, but you can do it on your own with any scenes you are learning.

5. <u>EXERCISE: STAYING AWAY FROM THE MATERIAL</u> (cont'd)

<u>Here's the exercise I do in class:</u> (requires a partner)

❖ Use a short scene and have a partner.

❖ Identify how you are really feeling right now.

❖ Do the *Follow the Feeling* exercise, but instead of saying how you feel say the line communicating *the feeling* instead of *the meaning*. Put how you feel *into* the words of the line.

❖ Your partner should be doing the same thing with his/her lines, so listen more to how he/she is feeling than to what he/she is saying.

❖ Allow your partner to affect you and put that feeling into your next line.

❖ Try to catch yourself if you're doing a *line reading*. Get back in touch with your feeling and try those words again.

❖ Don't edit yourself and don't think. Allow yourself to forget the words. If you have to *stop and think* about the words, you don't know the line well.

❖ If you forget a line, stay focused on your partner and make sounds; if the line is in there it will come to you.
   -- Do not look for the line on the ceiling, floor, or in your head. If you look for It, it will hide.

IF YOU DON'T LOOK FOR IT, IT WILL FIND YOU!

If the line doesn't come, you don't know it well enough. This exercise is also a good test of your knowing the lines or not. You should be able to say lines *without thinking* about them.

5. <u>EXERCISE: STAYING AWAY FROM THE MATERIAL</u> (cont'd)

<u>CAUTION!</u> **THIS IS JUST AN EXERCISE!** This is not how I propose you do your performances or auditions. It is for exploration purposes only. If you're comfortable with it, the spontaneity will show up in your work and feel *right.*

<u>What to look out for in the exercise:</u>

➢ It's best to listen more to *how* your partner is feeling than to *what* they are saying. Listening to the words will throw you back into the intelligence of the piece and you'll go back to intelligent line readings.

➢ It's okay to be wild and crazy with your feelings – even mock them up. It may also help if you can't find a feeling of your own, to mimic what your partner is feeling.

➢ It's easier to stay away from the material with bigger, even faked emotions or mimicking your partner, just to get the hang of the exercise.

➢ Once you have a handle on the basic idea, look for how you really are feeling and look for subtle changes. Use those feelings to color your words.

➢ Also stay away from literal references in the scene, such as the place, objects used, activities called for, etc. If you execute literal activity in the scene, you will more likely go back to the literal communication of the line. Example: if you're supposed to sit, stand up. Don't use appropriate gestures or props.

➢ If you notice you're being intelligent, ask yourself how that makes you feel and put that feeling into the line.

5. <u>EXERCISE: STAYING AWAY FROM THE MATERIAL</u> (cont'd)

<u>Here's the exercise at home:</u> (no partner needed)

❖ Use any material you are learning or have memorized.

❖ Identify how you are feeling right now, or pick an emotion to mock up.

❖ Do *Follow the Feeling*; but instead of saying how you feel say the line, communicating that feeling. Make the line all about *the feeling* you are having, not *the meaning* of the words.

❖ Keep using the feeling while you run the lines, or let it change if another feeling comes up.

❖ Try to catch yourself if you're doing a *line reading* and get back to how you are *feeling.*

❖ Use different stimulation each time you run the lines. Try singing them, using cartoon voices or being an animal of some kind. Try doing an activity that requires a change in rhythm: such as dancing, exercising, or cleaning.

❖ Don't think. If you have to stop what you're doing to think about what to say, you don't know the lines well enough. Go back and learn them.

❖ Notice new feelings you hadn't thought of before that could apply to the scene. Put them in your bag of *options*.

5. **EXERCISE: STAYING AWAY FROM THE MATERIAL** (cont'd)

Benefits of using this exercise:

- ✓ Helps you get used to reacting spontaneously.

- ✓ Helps you discover and allow more honest moments.

- ✓ Develops your ability to trust your impulses.

- ✓ Allows you to consider options for the scene you might not have thought of before.

- ✓ Develops your ability to have more attention on the external world and less attention on yourself.

- ✓ Helps you learn lines without learning a performance and keeps your line readings flexible.

- ✓ Exercises your ability to allow other characters in the scene to affect your performance.

- ✓ If nothing else, this exercise is a great test of whether or not you know your lines well enough so you don't have to think about them to remember them.

If you can get through the scene without having to think of what you're saying, you know the lines. If there are places in the scene where you have to stop and think, then you need to learn those lines better. If you are familiar with the "Italian" (speed) run of lines of theatre, you will get similar results with this exercise.

6. <u>HOW TO PREPARE IF THE SCENE IS EMOTIONALLY INTENSE</u>

Now that I've gotten you emotionally worked up, I'm going to remind you that intense emotion is not always called for in a scene. Yes, you need to be emotionally available, but only when necessary. As I've said earlier, not every scene is chockfull of emotional intensity. So, a word of caution -- don't look for places to be emotional in a scene just to show off your range.

Having said that, what if the audition scene *is* emotionally charged? How do you deal with getting yourself there? What if you have to be in an emotional state at the very beginning of the scene?

Here are some suggestions for preparing for this kind of emotionally charged audition scene:

-- **Don't panic.** Use the tools you know how to use and get to work on them. Panicking makes you tense up. *Emotions are released through relaxation.*

-- **The scene itself might bring up the right feelings.** If so, trust those feelings will be there; don't over-work the scene and diminish its impact on you.

-- If the material doesn't do it for you, **find a trigger or two** that most easily brings up the appropriate feeling: such as a piece of music, a personal life experience, sense memory, substitution, or a "what if..."

-- On the day of the audition, **you should put yourself in that mood** and stay close to it until the audition is done.

-- You can **use *Follow the Feeling*** as a warm-up to get yourself to where you need to be.

-- **Consider a few emotional options** that could work for you so you're not attached to just one feeling.

6. **HOW TO PREPARE IF IT IS EMOTIONALLY INTENSE** (cont'd)

Suggestions for preparing emotionally (cont'd)

-- **Pace yourself.** Don't peak too early. You want the energy and emotional explosion to come when you're in the audition, not before. Don't wear yourself out before you get there.

-- **Stay away from other distractions in your life** until the audition is over.

-- While you are waiting to go into the audition stay *in the zone.* Be private. Focus on the scene or your trigger. Don't chat.

-- When you get into the audition room stay *in the zone,* or **be neutral.** If they chat with you, don't let it affect the zone you're in for the scene.

Don't fake anything. Relax and let go. Use what you are really feeling.
Remember, there are lots of ways to feel that would be appropriate.
If you've thought of a few options, one of them should show up.
If you're not feeling anything, maybe the character is feeling numb.
Don't push it and don't fake a feeling.

 -- **Don't start the scene until you're ready.** Trust how you feel. If you're prepared, you'll be fine.

-- When you've done an emotional scene, **it may not be easy to just turn it off**. That's okay. Leave the audition room but stay in the waiting room until the residual feelings have quieted down.

-- Then **pat yourself on the back** for a job well done!

CHAPTER 4

CAMERA LOGISTICS:

Almost all professional auditions are on-camera now. The ease of the technology allows the decision makers to not only view the audition live, but also review it later. In many instances, the producer and director don't even come to the first round of auditions because they can view them anytime at their convenience. They might select actors of interest from the first tape and meet them in the call backs that are also usually recorded. Or they might cast the roles directly from the first round. It happens! I've also noticed producers and directors watching on computer screens, which may be streaming the auditions to other producers anywhere in the world.

So it's pretty important for an actor to be familiar with the logistics of how these on-camera sessions go:

- What does the room look like?
- Yiiiikes! There's a camera!
- Where do I go?
- Where do I look?
- Who is my scene partner?
- Can I move or do I stand still?
- What do I do for furniture?
- How *big* or *small* should I play it?
- Should I use props?

These are just a few of the questions I'm asked when I'm teaching or coaching. If you are going to be auditioning, you'd better know the answers. There seems to be a standard formula (with some variation) for setting up an audition room. Though every room is slightly different, the logistics for camera are usually the same.

You won't learn anything about these logistics in your scene study class unless you do some on-camera audition sessions. I'm going to go over all of these audition logistics so you will know what to expect.

If you want to actually work doing audition-style scene work with camera is every bit as important (if not more so) than studying any other aspect of acting. I don't care how talented you are. If you aren't comfortable and confident, if you are distracted by the audition atmosphere, you won't do your best work. It's not that you are bad at it; you're just uninformed and un-practiced working in that environment.

When I'm teaching audition technique, I set up my classroom to look like most professional on-camera audition situations. I focus on teaching students how to handle the logistics of working with camera as well as performance. There's a lot you can learn about what works and what doesn't, but you have to practice in front of a camera to be comfortable and confident in the audition room.

So here is what's usually in there:

1. **THE AUDITION ROOM:**

   - A camera (99% of the time)
   - Extra lighting (sometimes)
   - Extra standing microphone (sometimes)
   - A chair (or two) for the actor
   - A monitor (possibly just a computer)
   - Table and chairs, or sofa(s) and coffee table for auditors
   - A casting director
   - A camera operator
   - A reader (if casting director isn't doing it)
   - The actor's "mark"

See diagrams 1 & 2 on the next page:

diagram 1

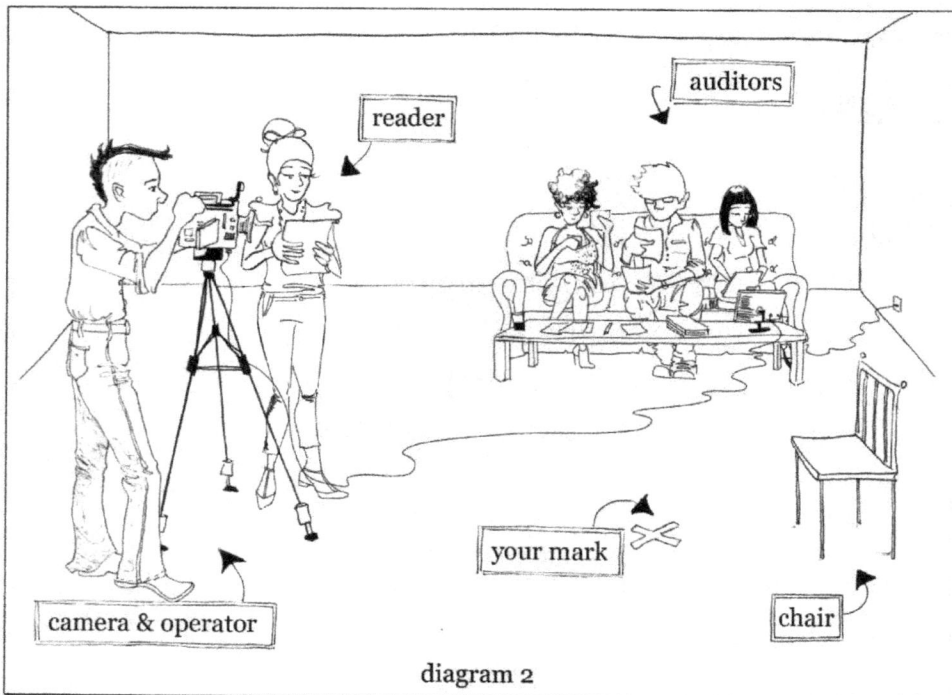

diagram 2

2. **FIND YOUR "MARK"**

First of all, you need to know what it is before you can find it.

A "mark" is an "X" or a "T" made with tape that's on the floor exactly where the casting director wants the actors to stand. When you enter the audition room, look for the mark and go there. (See diagrams #1 & #2)

If there is no tape, there may be a worn spot on the floor or carpet that *marks* the spot hundreds of actors have stood; go to that spot.

If there's no mark of any kind to be found usually standing in front of the camera is a good bet. The mark is always a good five or six feet away from the camera, so make sure you've got some distance between you and it. They set it up this way so that the camera operator can zoom in or out for a good shot. If you're too close to the camera, the focus may be off and they can't get a good close-up of you.

If you don't go there automatically when you enter, the casting director may say, "Take your mark." Now you'll know where to go.

3. **FIND THE "READER"**

First of all, who is the reader? It may be the Casting Director (some love to do it), or it may be an actor hired to be the reader. Some readers know what an actor needs and are great. Some either don't know, or aren't very good at giving you what you need. Be prepared for either. You should be able to get your work done regardless of the reader's ability. You can't blame them for your bad audition (many actors do). If they're not giving you what you need, get it from the words they are saying. If you're smart and paying attention to the reader, they sometimes can give a performance that helps yours enormously.

FIND THE READER (cont'd)

Unlike scene study class where your scene partner is on stage with you, in the audition there will be a reader who should be standing (or sitting) just off-camera. He/she will be reading the other role/roles in the scene for you. They should be next to one side of the camera or the other; if they aren't, ask them to go there. It will give you a good eye-line so the camera has a good shot of your face.

Your connection to the reader is your focus point in the scene. Never look directly into the camera unless you are talking to the audience. If you look into the camera, it looks like you are talking to the audience; or it establishes another person (besides the reader's character) in the scene.

How to handle different situations involving the reader:

-- **Two-character scene:** Make the reader your focus point.

-- **More than one character off-camera:** Occasionally, it happens that there is more than one other character in the scene; there are sometimes three or four. You usually only have one reader who will read all of those characters' lines. It could happen that you get more than one reader, but it's rare. Here's what to do when you only have one reader:

- Make the reader the character you talk to (or listen to) the most in the scene.
- Imagine that the other characters are next to the reader or on the other side of the camera.
- When preparing the scene, pay some attention to which character you need to be focusing on at any given moment. Learn this like you learn your lines.
- Trust that seeing imaginary people looks better than it feels.

OPTION NOTE: If you find it too confusing to place imaginary people, then use the reader as both characters, as long as you know whom you are talking to or listening to at any given moment.

FIND THE READER (cont'd)

-- **Phone call scenes:** When your character is on the phone, *do not look at the reader* if he/she is the character on the line. In fact, it will help to face away from the reader's side of the camera. Sometimes readers will help you out and turn their back to you; but even then, do not look at them. As soon as you glance at them, it puts that character in the room with you and not on the phone.

It may take focus and concentration to execute this. We are drawn to look toward the person talking, but resist the urge to do it; hear them through the phone and look at other things in the room.

-- **Car scenes:** Be mindful of positioning yourself and the reader to accommodate a driving situation:

If you are the driver, you want to face diagonally (45 degrees) to your *left* side of camera and have the reader sit off-camera to your *right*. Even though the distance feels strange, it looks like the passenger is sitting next to you. A word of caution – don't face too far to your left or you won't be seen.

If you are the passenger, do just the opposite of driving; face diagonally (45 degrees) to your *right*, and have the reader sit off-camera to your *left*.

If you are in a country that drives on the left side of the road, then *reverse* all of the above.

-- **Travelling the reader:** Occasionally, the actor needs to see the off-camera character move. He/she comes in, or leaves, or crosses the room, or approaches from a distance, etc. You may or may not be able to have the reader move for you. If not, you need to imagine the character travelling and actually follow the imaginary person with your eyes. It can be tricky, so I recommend doing it only if it is absolutely necessary for the execution of your scene.

4. TO MOVE, OR NOT TO MOVE

It's okay to move. In fact I recommend it. After all, it is called the Motion Picture business. Moving (or not) should depend on your choice of where you are, what you are doing, and activity suggested by the scene itself.

You can make some moves you feel are necessary in order to execute the scene properly. However, audition rooms can be small, and you don't want to make the camera operator's job too tricky.

Occasionally, you might be asked to just sit and read the scene. If that's the case, just make the adjustment and do what is requested; otherwise, feel free to execute some actions.

It will help if you're aware of the following:

- Limit yourself to 2 or 3 steps in either direction.
- Moving upstage (away from camera) is fine, but don't go downstage (toward the camera) past the mark.
- Sitting down or standing up during the scene is okay.
  Do it slowly, so the camera can follow you. Even if you should be moving quickly – *hurry slowly*.
- Always let the camera operator know if you are going to be making any moves, so he/she can be ready to follow you.

Yes, you can enter or exit a scene as well. Here are some options:

- If you want to enter, come from off left or off right of the mark. Remember, a few steps and you are off camera.
- If you're already on camera and want to step up to someone, come from directly upstage of your mark.
- If the person you're talking to is following you, come from downstage (next to camera) to your mark.

NOTE: It's okay to start with your back to the camera. The entrance looks great and as soon as you get to your mark you can turn around before you talk.

TO MOVE OR NOT TO MOVE (cont'd)

Here are some other tips regarding movement:

Often the actions called for in a scene can't be executed fully because of the logistical limitations of the audition space. The same applies to interactions with the other character in the scene. It's perfectly okay to compromise those activities or maybe even lose them altogether. For example:

Walking and talking scenes: Some scenes are set outdoors and the characters are walking on the street or in a park. Since you can't be walking, you can enter and then *stop* and have the conversation. At the end of the conversation, continue walking and exit. Your *place* (street or park) should remain the same. Remember to exit in the opposite direction – unless you're going back in that direction for a reason.

Handing something to/taking something from the character off camera: In most audition spaces the reader is too far away for you to reach easily. You don't want to leave your mark and be off-camera to hand something to them or get something from them. If you are close enough to them without leaving your mark then do it. Make sure you let them know what you're going to do, and make sure you remember to give them the thing you want them to hand you. If you're not close enough, you can put a chair directly in front of you and pick up (put down) the thing you are getting (giving).

Physical interaction with the other character: First of all, most readers do *not* want to be touched. Do it only if you have their permission. Many times a scene demands physical contact: such as a fight, or a kiss, etc. What do you do? If you can think of a way to compromise this situation, do that. For instance:
If it's *a **hug or kiss***, intend the feeling of wanting or having one. Don't kiss or hug the air. You can ignore the activity if it isn't that necessary.

TO MOVE OR NOT TO MOVE (cont'd)

Physical interaction: (cont'd)

If it's a *fight scene*, check with the casting director first about how he/she wants to execute the fight. Be prepared to throw yourself around or fake being hit; you might have to do it. If so, do the minimum and don't do anything to cause yourself injury. Don't damage the furniture or anything in the room either. They usually don't expect an actor to do anything requiring stunt work, unless you are a stunt performer.

If it is a *car scene*, I've already covered these logistics in the *Find the Reader* section, but there are some other things to consider:

-- If the scene isn't all about actually driving (even if you're supposed to be driving) then pretend you've *parked the car* and have the conversation.

-- If you are talking about actually driving, make sure you are watching the road and don't steer too much. I suggest you just keep your hands on your lap as if you're holding the bottom of the wheel and steer from there; or put a chair in front of you and use the back of the chair as a wheel. It looks better than holding an imaginary steering wheel.

On opening and closing imaginary doors: *Don't do it*. If you are answering a door, you can pretend the door is open; step onto your mark from off-camera and imagine that you are in a doorway. If you are closing a door, just step out of your imaginary doorway. If you are supposed to slam the door in someone's face, then you may have to mime it. When you come into a scene, don't close a door behind you; you will probably forget to open it when you leave and you'll walk *through* the door. Again, pretend it's already open when you enter, and leave it open when you exit.

On knocking on imaginary doors: *Don't do it.* You can begin with standing at the door, waiting for it to open and use this as your moment before.

TO MOVE OR NOT TO MOVE (cont'd)

A WORD OF CAUTION

If you *must knock* then make sure you have a chair or a wall to knock on. *Do not* knock on air while you stamp your foot!

If the scene requires you to *leave briefly and come back,* do that. Step out of frame (a step or two is sufficient) and come back *immediately.* Don't wait the length of real time it would take to do the off-camera business, otherwise the camera will be rolling on *empty* space. Make the move quickly.

5. BE SEEN/BE HEARD

When you are planning your activity for a scene you must design your moves so that the camera can see your face 98% of the time. Don't let yourself face away from the camera for too long or look down too much, particularly if you're sitting, driving, or you're on the phone. You can look away and look down occasionally; it is normal, human behavior to do that as long as you remember the 98% rule.

If you are **sitting** it might be a good idea to have the reader standing (if that works for the scene).

If you are **standing** it will be better if the reader is standing. If they must sit, remember to keep your eye line as high as possible.

If you are **on the phone** and you are on a speaker phone that is on your desk, remember to keep your eye line high; don't bend over too much.

If you are **on the phone** and using a cell phone (which is recommended), always put the phone to your *upstage* ear (in the hand away from the camera), otherwise the phone and your hand will block your face. Use the ear that is most comfortable for you, and then face in the direction that puts the phone *upstage.* *Remember to turn the phone completely off!*

BE SEEN/BE HEARD: (cont'd)

...If you are **on the phone...**

-- Try to get the reader positioned on the opposite side of the camera from the side you are facing. You'll be better able to look around the room without catching a glimpse of the reader.

-- Look up! We tend to look down when we talk on the phone. Since the auditors want to see your face, remind yourself to look around the room while you talk, not at the floor. This is particularly important if you're sitting down.

It is also very important that you make yourself *heard* as well as seen. If you're trained in theatre this probably won't be a problem. If you haven't had voice training, you should consider getting some.

Yes, you want to be naturally conversational in the scene; but if you are a soft-spoken person in life, you may not be loud enough to be heard across an audition room. The microphone is usually in the camera, which can be some distance from you.

Scenes require an energy that is a little more intense than real life. If you are loud enough your energy is also probably right. Between the setup of the room and the energy necessary for the scene, it may not seem as intimate as you would like to make it, but get used to it. You don't want the audience to have to work hard just to hear you.

The same thing applies to those of you who are *fast talkers*. You know who you are. You must learn to s-l-o-w-d-o-w-n and a-r-t-i-c-u-l-a-t-e.

If either of these issues apply to you, voice training is probably necessary. Unless you are highly self-disciplined, you are going to need help. Voice class will help with breathing, articulation, volume, vocal control and even emotional expression. So do yourself a favor, and take a class.

6. PLAY THE SIZE ROOM YOU'RE IN

Remembering this rule will help with your being seen and heard. I'm frequently asked: "How big should I be?", or an actor will say, "I've been told I'm too big, so I'm trying to be small." My reply is, "Play the size of the room you're in."

If you are on stage you need to reach the back wall of the theatre. If you're on camera you need to reach the reader next to the camera (where the mic is). Stage requires a bigger voice and bigger movement; camera requires less. However, there are *two* rooms you need to consider for camera:

The room in the scene:

Our environment always affects our communication and physical expression. There's a difference between having an intimate conversation in your living room or bedroom and one that takes place at a party, a bar, in a boardroom, or in an office. Are you talking to just one person, or addressing a crowd at a rally? Your awareness of your surroundings and other circumstances should also alter your vocal level and your behavior.

The audition room you are in:

Think of the reader (camera) as your focal point. If you reach the reader with your voice, you reach the camera (mic) and the audience. You don't have to worry about how *big* or how *small* you are being; just worry about being truthful. If your emotion is honestly intense, be big and intense; it will work as long as it's real.

NOTE:

My observation of the *big vs. small* issue is not a *big* or *small* one, but a *real vs. fake* one. I hate it when an actor is told that he/she is "too big" on camera. What that usually means is that they aren't being *real*. They are *faking* it. If you fake it on camera it looks too *big.* You can get away with a lot more on stage than you can on film. As a result, actors who have a stage background tend to have a problem with *too big*, which leads me to my next point:

7. THE CAMERA SEES ALL!

The camera is an objective witness to what you are doing and feeling. If the character is in a highly emotional state and is all worked up, then go there: but you must be really feeling the emotion. If you're faking it, the camera sees that and it looks *too big*. There's nothing worse than watching someone cry or yell when they aren't really sad or angry. I'm sure you've seen it, as I have, and it's embarrassing to watch.   The camera knows they're faking and so does the audience.

I also have a theory that the camera can't see what you're *thinking*, but always sees how you are *feeling.* An actor has two levels of awareness: one as the actor, and another as the character. The good news is that the camera won't see what you (the actor) are thinking: the bad news is that the camera will see feelings generated by your *actor* thoughts. So you must let your *actor* feelings be the character's feelings, because like it or not, the camera is going to see them!

NOTE: The camera is a useful tool if you can get past judging yourself. What you think is being successfully communicated and what the audience is getting might be two entirely different things.

I use a camera in my classes almost all the time for two reasons:

-- So that actors get used to working in front of it:

- ✓ Putting a scene *on its feet* in front of a camera is quite different than just *visualizing* how you'll do it.

- ✓ Practicing frequently in front of the camera makes you more comfortable in that environment.

- ✓ Once you get past your judgments, you can see what works and what doesn't.

THE CAMERA SEES ALL! (cont'd)

-- <u>So that actors can watch "playback" and observe:</u>

    ✓ What they did or didn't do.

    ✓ What does and what doesn't work for camera.

    ✓ How certain movements, while feeling a bit
       unreal, actually look fine on camera.

I must confess I have my own agenda for using camera in class as well. It comes in very handy when I comment on something an actor does and he/she says, "I didn't do that." I can say, "Oh yes you did. Let's watch it."

You've also heard the old adage, "A picture is worth a thousand words". How true it is! When actors watch themselves they see what works and what doesn't. Often, I don't even have to comment; they fix what didn't work by themselves.

Working out on-camera on a regular basis teaches students how to use the camera to their advantage, and they become very comfortable working in front of it. However, the most valuable aspect is the playback, as they can't be watching what they are doing while they are in the scene.

I highly recommend owning a camera yourself, practicing in front of it, and watching playback; just make sure you are practicing the right stuff.

Now that I've made you very aware of the camera, I'm going to tell you to:

8. <u>FORGET THE CAMERA</u>

The analysis you do on a scene, practicing, learning the lines, the training you've had in class, even reading this book – *everything* you do to prepare for an on-camera audition – will allow you to **forget the camera is there when you're in the audition.**

All of your thoughts, your focus and attention, are now on being the character in the scene. Any thoughts about camera, director, casting director, nerves, booking the role, etc., are not going to help you get the job done.

If you're solidly prepared, just focus all of your attention on your *place*, *moment before* and *listening* to the reader, then a wonderful thing can happen. It's as if a veil comes down between you and the reader, and the rest of the room! You're totally unaware of the existence of anything but the life of the character. When it's over, you barely remember even doing it. That's usually a good thing. It's called being in the scene and getting the job done.

As I say in class, "Once you start the scene, everything that happens to you happens to the character".

    -- If *you* drop something, the *character* drops something.

    -- If *you* fall off the chair, the *character* falls off the chair.

So forget the camera; forget that you're auditioning, just live the character's life.

As you become more experienced, these things become easier to do; that's why practicing is so important. You are less likely to be thrown by things that go wrong and you can turn them into *happy accidents*. The only difference between a beginner and an experienced professional is that a beginner is trying to *be perfect*; while the professional knows there's a good chance that's not going to happen and has learned to make the most of it.

9. PROPS

Some casting directors and directors are of the opinion that you should *never* use props in an audition. I beg to differ. I think they probably have had terrible experiences watching actors fumbling with props, or having had actors waste their valuable time setting up elaborate props and then not using them at all.

For example:

An actor decides to take keys out of his jacket pocket in the scene. He's arguing with the other character, wants to grab his keys and storm out of the room; but he hasn't practiced with the jacket and keys beforehand. So in the audition, he reaches in his pocket to get the keys; out comes not only the keys, but a hand full of *pocket junk* – candy wrappers, old tissues, and lint. Having to deal with all of that, he blows the end of the scene and loses his audience, who are laughing and more interested in what's coming out of his pocket.

Another example:

An actress decides to be loading up her purse while talking to the other character in the scene. When she gets into the room and they say, "go ahead", she starts to unload all of the stuff in her purse. The auditors wait while she gets her keys, wallet, hair brush, cell phone, and make-up out of her purse and has to decide where to put it all. She starts the scene *and doesn't load her purse* while she's talking. She has just pissed off the auditors, who are now thinking, "What were we waiting for? She didn't use anything she took all that time to set up!"

I believe that sometimes using a prop is absolutely necessary in order to maintain the reality of the scene for the actor as well as the audience. But a prop is not always necessary for an audition even if the script mentions it. You need to decide what you *must have* and what you *don't really need* to fulfill your life in the scene.

PROPS: (cont'd)

Here are some questions to guide you through making the decision to use a prop or not. Ask yourself:

- Do I talk about what's in my hand?
    Example: "I have to bounce her like this, or she cries."
    Solution: Wrap up your jacket and use as a baby.

- Does another character talk about what I'm holding?
    Example: "Flowers! Are they for me? Thank you!"
    Solution: Bring some fake flowers.

- Do I have to give someone something in the scene?
    Example: "Here's my business card."
    Solution: Hand the reader a card or piece of paper.
            If you can't reach them put it on a chair in front of you,
            or just drop it off camera.

- Does another character give you something in the scene?
    Example: "Take this file home with you."
    Solution: Give paper or file folder to reader, ask them to
            hand it to you. If they can't reach you, put it on
            a chair in front of you and pick it up.

- Is there an activity I must do for my sense of the reality
  and rhythm of the scene?
    Example: I need to grab my purse and dig my keys out
            in frustration.
    Solution: Bring your purse; know where those keys are
            in the bag, but pretend to hunt for them.

PROPS: (cont'd)

Ask yourself: (cont'd)

- Is the prop I need too big and complicated to bring and use?
  <u>Example</u>: I should be working on my computer...
  <u>Solution</u>: Mime that activity.

- Can I live a full life in the scene without using what the script suggests?
  <u>Example</u>: I'm supposed to be cleaning up in the kitchen.
  <u>Solution #1</u>: Answer is no, I'm bringing a dish rag.
  <u>Solution #2</u>: Answer is yes, the scene has nothing to do with cleaning up.

If you must use a prop, here are some rules you should follow:

❖ **Always practice using the prop before your audition.**

-- Props seem to have a life of their own. You need to figure out how the prop is going to behave when you are preparing the scene:

- when to pick it up
- which hand to use
- when and where to put it down
- managing my script and the prop at the same time.

You don't want to find out in the middle of the audition that the prop doesn't work the way you *thought* it would. A little practice goes a long way!

PROPS: (cont'd)

❖ Keep it simple!

-- Just use what you need to handle. This is not scene study class so you don't need to dress the set.

-- Work it out so the prop is serving you in the most minimal way possible. Don't make it a scene about a prop.

-- If what the script suggests is too complicated, minimalize what you need for the audition.

-- If the scene is a phone call, use your cell phone and make sure it's completely *turned off*.

❖ The prop doesn't have to be the real thing.

- If you're at a bar and drinking, use a bottle of water.
- If you're looking at papers, use your sides.
- If you're holding a baby, wrap up a sweater or jacket.
- If you *must* eat, make it a yogurt, a cracker or chips.

REMEMBER:
DON'T SET UP PROPS AND THEN NOT USE THEM
ALWAYS PRACTICE WITH THEM FIRST

CHAPTER 5

MIRACLE MONOLOGUE

This is a technique for teaching actors how to learn their lines quickly when preparing an audition. Often you'll get the audition call the day before you are to go in and you'll get the sides late in the day when the audition is the first thing in the morning. Now and then you'll have a couple of days to prep. You may get lucky and be called on Friday for a Monday audition which gives you the weekend to prepare; that's the exception to the rule.

If you're auditioning for an "actor" (five lines) role you may only have a page to learn. If it's a large "principal" (over 10 lines) role you could have 10 pages, or more, involving 2 to 4 scenes. Many actors prefer to work without the sides in the audition and for good reason, but how do you learn it all on such short notice?

Actors want to learn their lines because they don't want to cold read; the sides get in their way. They feel freer without it and their performance is better when they're not tied to the pages of the script. Although that's true there's a difference between how well they *think* they know the lines and how well they *actually* know them.

Most actors have been trained to get the words right, so they try to learn the exact words. At home where it is quiet they are word perfect, but the pressure of the audition throws them. Suddenly they are so worried about getting the words right they start forgetting them, or they look like they are trying to remember lines, instead of living the life of the character.

What actors don't know is that the auditors (directors, producers, etc.) don't really care about your getting every word right. In fact, at this point in the process even the writers don't know the exact words. What they care about now is your understanding of the scene, your fit with this character, your look, your qualities, and their confidence in you as an actor. So it's just not worth sacrificing your performance trying to remember the right words.

1. **LEARNING LINES QUICKLY**

I call this the *Miracle Monologue* because I hand out monologues to my students, give them the rules, give them 15 minutes to learn the lines and get them up on camera. They do the piece twice – once cold reading and once from memory. Some of the pieces are quite long.

Many of the students don't think they will be able to do the monologue with only 15 minutes to learn it, but if they follow my rules all of them get through it. They think it's a miracle, but it's really just applying the technique.

In fact, I've found that most actors are more word perfect *without* the sides than when they cold-read the piece. That's because when we rely on the paper we stop thinking. We don't try to remember what we know. We glance at the words without really seeing them and we screw it up. Without the sides we *must think* about what we are saying; when we allow ourselves to think, we remember all of the right words.

This technique has worked for hundreds of actors, many of whom have thanked me for it over the years. It's actually very simple and it works *if you follow the rules*:

Rule #1 -- Don't panic.

- ❖ Sounds silly but truly it's a rule. *Tell yourself you can do it.*
- ❖ If you tell yourself you can't, you won't. Panic is never a helpful condition; it keeps you from focusing on the work and getting the job done.

Rule #2 -- Learn the *thought line** through the piece.

- ❖ Read the piece through at least 10 times to get the story.

- ❖ Do not try to memorize the *right* words.

- ❖ Then learn **key words and phrases*…
  - ▪ Memorize the list of key words/phrases in the order that they appear in the scene.
  - ▪ Go over that list without looking at the paper.
  - ▪ First I talk about (key word/words), then I talk about (key phrase).

- ❖ When you learn the thought line, the other words in the line seem to fall into place by themselves.

- ❖ You also know what it is you are talking about. I call it *owning the story*. (See next page)

Rule #3 – Focus and Concentrate

- ❖ *Use your prep time well.* Focus on the task at hand.

- ❖ Concentrate on the key words, phrases and the story.

- ❖ Do not let your mind wander while you stare at the page. I can stare at the piece of paper in my hand for 15 minutes, but my mind can be a million miles away. I am not preparing; I just *look* like I am.

- ❖ If you catch yourself drifting off, bring yourself back to the task of learning the thought line.

Rule #3 – Focus and Concentrate (cont'd)

Owning the story:

If you memorize the lines by rote, you are learning unrelated words; you won't have a sense of their meaning as a whole. You have no understanding of the communication. If you forget a word you can't replace it with a word that means the same thing because you don't have a context for that word.

If you learn the *thought line,* you are learning the whole story. You have a context; you know what you are talking about. If you had to, you could tell the whole story in your own words. I call that *owning the material.*

I spend a good deal of time when I'm coaching just helping actors learn lines. Some actors are well aware of their need to understand what they are talking about; they know it will make learning the lines easier. Some actors are in too much of a hurry or don't think it's necessary and have more trouble remembering their lines. If an actor continues to miss the same line when we are running the scene, I know he/she hasn't grasped the meaning yet. Once they know the thought they are communicating, they have no trouble remembering it.

If you want to be a *good* actor you must always own what you're saying. You can't really communicate unless you grasp the meaning and you understand the message you are delivering. If you don't know what you are talking about the audience isn't going to know either.

2. <u>MAKING IT UP</u>

The second half of the *Miracle Monologue* exercise is to do the piece on camera twice. For the first take, students have the script in hand and do a cold read, making sure they are getting the words right. The students then put the script down and do the piece from memory. I give them a second set of rules to follow on this second take:

Rule #1 – Don't panic (See previous Rule #1)

Rule #2 – Focus and Concentrate (See previous Rule #3)

Rule #3 – Make it up

❖ *Think* your way through it.

❖ Take your time.

❖ If you forget a word, use one that means the same thing.

❖ If you forget all the words of a line but you know the thought, *make it up.* Say it in your own words.

❖ Once you start the piece, you can't stop and start over.

The results of this exercise always astound the students who have just performed a page-long monologue from memory after 15 minutes of preparation.

When we view the tape, they see that they were more accurate and the overall performances were better without the script; which is why actors prefer to work without the script in the first place. It's crazy, though, to try to work without the script if you don't really own those lines well enough to make it up.

"Don't we need to get the words right in the audition?" *No, you don't!* As long as the key elements of the lines are there; even if you change a few words, skip a line, reverse the order of some phrases, or say something in your own words that means the same thing, the auditors really don't care.

NOTE: This applies only to film and TV auditions. In commercial auditions, you must be word perfect!

Trust me. I've changed words, skipped lines and just plain made up speeches over the course of my auditioning life. To this day no one has ever yelled at me. I've even apologized a few times when I thought I'd changed too much, but most of the time they didn't even notice (I should have kept my mouth shut!).

Unless the casting director has requested that you memorize the scene, which rarely happens, the auditors don't expect you to know it all that well. In fact, they wonder why you don't just read it if you're not confident with the lines.

There are some casting directors who have been spoiled by actors who always memorize the lines, whether asked to or not. So they might have expectations. If they ask why you don't know the lines tell them you're not confident enough to do it without the script. You might also mention you weren't asked to have it memorized, otherwise you certainly would have. (I've been around so long, if they said anything to me I'd mention they aren't paying me enough to learn the lines yet, but that's me.)

What Directors, Producers and Casting Directors *do* have a right to expect is that you have *prepared* the scene. That's entirely different from learning the lines. They expect you have an understanding of what's going on and are bringing your unique interpretation to the scene, but that has nothing to do with learning lines. If you just learn the words and don't own the material, you won't know what you're talking about and be more likely to forget the words anyway. Many actors make this mistake, but you won't, will you!

3. ALWAYS CARRY THE SCRIPT

As I've said, there are benefits to auditioning without having the sides in your hand and most actors prefer to work this way because:

- You're freer physically.
- Your connection to the reader is better.
- You own what you're saying because you have to think about it.
- When you have to think, natural pauses happen that can be brilliant.

But you must be confident about your communication and not have any attention on getting the words right or you will ruin your audition.

I have always maintained that you *must* carry the script into the room with you. It reminds them that this is a work in progress not a finished product. Sometimes you might forget a line because of a real moment you are having in the scene. You don't want to have to stop at what might be your best moment because you don't have your script handy.

You should:

- ✓ Carry that script in with you. Either have it in your hand, or put it down nearby, so if you need it you can get to it easily.
- ✓ Think your way through *as if* you don't have the script.
- ✓ If you do blank and can't make it up, take a look at the script. Do it only after giving yourself a chance to remember.
- ✓ Once you get the line, get off the page again and think your way through the rest of the scene.

NOTE: If you have the script in your hand you will be tempted to look at it. Resist that temptation unless you blank. If you use it before you need it, you will stop thinking your way through and be forced to use the paper for the rest of the scene.

CHAPTER 6

COLD READ

1. SOMETIMES YOU MUST

As much as I love the *Miracle Monologue* technique and auditioning without the paper, there are times when it's not possible to learn the lines beforehand.

- ➢ You might get the sides too late.
- ➢ There is too much material to learn with confidence in the time you have to prepare.
- ➢ You might get the *wrong* sides -- it happens.
- ➢ After you've auditioned, they ask you to read another scene that you haven't seen before.
- ➢ They give you a different role to look at when you're at the audition and give you only a few minutes to look it over.
- ➢ They give you a different role to do while you're in the room and ask you to just cold read it.

What do you do then? If you have a solid cold reading technique, it shouldn't be a problem.

I have had to cold read in auditions and been very grateful that I was comfortable enough to do it without damaging my performance. If they know you haven't had time to prepare and you do a really good job, the auditors are very impressed. If they like you enough to work with you further you don't want to blow it just because you have to cold read.

Work on developing your cold reading ability. It is a key component of your skill set. Following are some rules to help you with your cold reading technique. You will thank me for it one day.

2. <u>STEPS TO FOLLOW</u>

It is important to be conversational even though you are reading. We read out loud differently than when we speak to a person. When we read we sound like we are talking <u>at</u> someone. When we communicate we are talking <u>to</u> someone. Even though you are reading a scene you want to sound like you are talking <u>to</u> someone, <u>not at</u> them.

– Never look at your script while the other character is talking.

Listen to what the reader is saying first. You have time to look at your line when they are finished. I know it feels as if a long time goes by, but it doesn't take much time at all.

– Look down, get your line, then look up and talk.

Connect to the reader before you start talking. If you have to deliver a long speech, keep re-connecting with the reader every now and then; it will help keep your *reading* conversational.

– Connect to the reader when you get to the end of your speech.

So that you are sure you are *listening* again.

– Stay connected to your whole body.

Don't let having the paper in your hand shut you down physically. Do what you can to have at least a minimal physical existence in the scene.

– Practice, practice, practice!

Do lots of cold reads. Read material out loud as if you are talking to someone; read scenes, newspapers, even read a novel. It's really the only way to get there. Follow the rules and practice.

CHAPTER 7

ONE-LINERS

1. IT'S STILL A SCENE

Every scene has its own degree of difficulty. You might think that the longer, or more complicated the scene is the more difficult it would be. I believe the opposite is true. I believe the most difficult scene is actually the *one-liner*.

It looks so simple, but that's what makes it the most difficult. Most actors don't think they need to do anything with the one line, or maybe they don't know *what* to do. Actors also get a bit cocky about making *sure* they've learned the words. After all it's just *one* line – how hard could it be?

I've seen it happen more than once in class. It's easier to remember three pages of dialogue than it is to remember that one line. Early in my career, I had one of those auditions myself. I forgot my two words!

A one-liner is also awkward and uncomfortable to audition for because it's short, and it's pretty much over before you know what's happened. Psychologically it's such a *small* role and it doesn't look like a full scene. Ah, but it is a full scene! If you treat it as such, it will be much more comfortable for you in the audition.

There are probably more one-line roles to read for than other size parts, especially when you are just getting started as a professional. The casting directors know that you're green (inexperienced). They think that one-liners are easy, so they bring you in for those. Since they're *not* easy, it's best to know how to prepare for them.

The most important thing to remember is that *it is still a scene:*
>   -- It has a beginning (moment before)
>   -- It has a middle (fighting for, relationship, etc.)
>   -- It has an end (moment after)

IT'S STILL A SCENE (cont'd)

You need to make choices and give the character a life, just as you would for any scene. You can pretend that it's a much larger role and you only have one line in this scene, or remind yourself there are no *small* roles, only *small* actors. This might help you overcome your resistance to doing such a small role.

Years ago, I read for a character that only had one line. It turned out to be recurring role in the series, but in the first episode she only one line. Fortunately, I knew what to do with that one line. I booked the job and did five out of six episodes. Most of the time, it's one line in one episode of the show. You still should do your best. It's an opportunity to show the auditors what you can do, especially if you are just starting out and meeting the casting director for the first time.

Here's an example of what a one-liner looks like: (written by Henry Mah)
(Role of the "Flight Attendant")

```
8 INT. AIRPLANE PASSENGER AREA - NIGHT                    8

A flight attendant is knocking on the door of the washroom.

                    FLIGHT ATTENDANT
          Sir, I'll have to ask you to return
          to your seat, please.

                    BILL
          (from inside washroom)
          Thanks. I'll just be a minute.

The flight attendant begins to push a refreshment cart down
the aisle.
                                        CUT TO:
```

It's *one* line; make sure you can remember it!

2. **DON'T ELABORATE**

Because the one-liner is so short, actors want to expand the role in their performance. They decide to make up a whole life for this character and add all sorts of twists and turns to the scene to enrich the role. They give the character a full-on back story they've made up, that has nothing to do with why this character exists.

Please note: *the character exists to say this one line*. The character lives only at this particular moment, in this particular scene, for a singular and particular reason. Your job is to know what that is, do only that, and do it well.

Resist the urge to over-do it. Don't elaborate. Keep it simple and to the point. Don't pad your part. My motto for any audition (and especially for one-liners) is, "Simple...executed brilliantly".

It will be good enough if you live in the moment, are honest, and take care of the business at hand. Yes, it can feel awkward and uncomfortable and even downright silly to do a one-liner. Know that it always look better than it feels — that should give you some comfort.

Simple...
executed brilliantly!

3. <u>MY THEORY</u>

When casting a one-liner, I think the auditors are more concerned with *physical type* than they are with *audition performance*. Not that a good performance doesn't count – it's just not as important as the physical statement this character needs to make in the few seconds of screen time he/she will have.

It will be such a brief moment, there's no time to develop the character's personality; so how the actor *looks* needs to say a lot.

Because it's only one line, an actor's ability is not as much of an issue as it is with a larger role. In this case a *less able* performer who is *more the right type* will probably get the role. Auditors are pretty sure they can get the actor who looks right to do at least *one* good take of the one line.

Don't worry about not getting a one-line role. It probably wasn't what you did; you just weren't the right physical type. Knowing this, you should still do your best and show them how talented you are. If you don't get this role and you're good, the casting director will notice and see you for another project, or maybe even give you an opportunity to read for a larger role in this one.

Section Two: The Mastery of Auditioning

Purpose of an audition:

1) To entertain them

2) To show them your stuff

When you go into an audition, remind yourself of what you are there to accomplish: what you are there to **give** not what you are there to **get**. The preparation needed to be all about you, now the audition should be all about *them*. Of course you want to get the job, but that is not ultimately in your control. You need to focus on what *is* in your control which is *executing the audition well.*

Remember, this is the entertainment business. My theory is that if you can *entertain* the auditors, they know you can entertain the audience; so be there to entertain them. Transport them from the arduous task of casting to the relaxing position of being entertained.

It's also called show business. You are there to *show* them what you can do with this role. Show them:
-- you have the ability, you understand the material, and you can deliver.
-- what this role looks like on you.
-- how well you can take directions and that you'd be fun to work with.
-- what you look like on film.

CHAPTER ONE

PREPARING AT HOME

We get to work harder than most people who have only one job to worry about. Actors have two careers: one (J-O-B) that gives them an income and one (acting) that *might* give them an income. Actors have to juggle their *actual* duties and responsibilities with their *potential* acting careers.

There's a great deal that goes into getting ready for an audition. Hours of preparation at home, the time spent getting there, waiting to be seen, and finally auditioning. Regardless of how much or how little time you have to do it, you still have to prepare.

When that audition call comes, whether you have a few days or not, you may need to make this your priority and get right to work on the following:

1. Read the script

If you have access to the full script, find the time to read it. The full script will give you all the information you need to understand your character. It will give you your character's place in the whole picture: background, relationship information, and a sense of the overall tone of the piece.

If the script isn't available, or you don't have time to read it, don't worry. Everything you really need to know is in the scenes you've been given. If you get all the character's breakdowns, read them. Reading the breakdowns will give you a pretty good idea about the whole story, especially if you didn't read the script.

Read your scene or scenes carefully over and over, just to get the information. Don't start saying lines out loud until you have a full understanding of what each scene is about.

If you start talking too soon you're in danger of locking into line readings before you know what's going on, or before you understand the true meaning of what you're saying in the context of the whole scene.

Read each scene at least 10 times. If there is anything you don't fully understand, read it another 10 times. Stick with it until you get it and you're confident you understand the scene.

2. Don't start acting yet

Start making choices once you've read and understand the scene. Don't start saying lines out loud yet. Make choices based on the *12 Choices* I've covered in Chapter 2.

Remember, the first 6 choices apply to every scene so make sure you have those covered. Be clear about them, particularly what you're *Fighting For* (objective). Some scenes are tough to figure out. Don't get lazy about it; stay with it until you have clear, specific choices in all six areas.

Then consider if any of the second six choices apply. They may or may not fit, but consider them all anyway. Be careful not to force any of these choices onto a scene just to cover your bases; if it doesn't apply, don't use it.

After you've made your choices, ask yourself which ones will help you the most with this particular scene. I call these *operative choices*. There may be one, two, or even three choices you've made that clearly *drive* this scene and will help you the most in your analysis.

For instance, it may be all about the *relationship* between the two people talking in the scene, with at least three *events* in it as well. The *operative choices*, in this case, would be *relationship* and *events*. In another scene, *where* it takes place may be very important, and there's a good deal of hiding information between the characters. In this case, *place* and *mystery and secret* would be the *operative choices*.

Having a firm grasp of these choices will help clarify your understanding and assist in your execution of the scene. Once you have gotten through this part, tedious but necessary, the rest of the preparation should be easier and more fun.

3. Put the scene "on its feet"

Now you're ready to start acting. You can put the scene "on its feet", meaning:

- ✓ You can start talking out loud and learning the lines.
- ✓ You can visualize and map out your physical life.
- ✓ You can set the framework for how you will execute the scene.
- ✓ You can get out of your chair, walk and talk through the scene and get a feel for how you might want to do it. Even if it's a sitting-down scene, put yourself in an appropriate chair and imagine the environment around you.

My suggestion is that you actually stage the scene as if you were in the audition room. Use your imagination and set up the physical environment of the audition room at home. Imagine where the camera is, where the reader will be, where you will be standing or sitting. Use your choices (place, moment before, etc.) to set up the environment in the scene and work out how you're going to do it.

4. Practice, practice, practice

Go over the lines and your character's physical life until you feel comfortable and the scene flows smoothly. Rehearse with any props you might want to use. Props have a way of taking on a life of their own. If you're going to use them you must practice with them *before* going into the audition. You need to know how that prop is going to behave and how to handle it in order to make it work.

If something feels awkward or uncomfortable, *now* is the time to fix it. You don't want to find out when you're in the actual audition that your good idea feels terrible and doesn't work because you didn't try it out.

Once you've got the framework in place and it feels right, commit to it. Don't overwork the scene or second guess your choices; leave it alone and clean up any loose ends with regard to the lines. Don't worry about whether or not what you're going to do is what the casting director, producer or director will want. As long as you're satisfied with what you are doing, be confident and committed.

5. <u>Commit to choices/find your "hook"</u>

If you are certain there is information missing that is critical to your understanding of the scene, be sure to find out from someone who would know before you go or when you get to the audition. Probably what you *think* it's about is what it *is* about. Most film and TV scenes are not that deep. Commit to your choices.

You can make even bad choices work by committing to them 100%.

If you're not 100% committed, even great choices won't work.

If you're feeling doubtful and having trouble committing to a choice, change it. Find another choice that makes you more comfortable and go with it 100%.

If you are having difficulty getting the scene to flow easily, even though your choices are logical and appropriate, you may be missing what I call the hook. The hook is what's going to pull it all together and help you to be in complete ownership of the character's situation. It may be a piece of information that you've missed, something you've misinterpreted, or something going on in the scene that you haven't considered. There's a key element you sense you're not getting.

When this happens to me I know I must keep searching, thinking about it, re-reading the scene, digging a little deeper to find the hook; and if I don't, I'll be uncomfortable in the audition. When I find that hook (sometimes in the car on the way to the audition) I know it. I can feel it come together. Everything just makes that much more sense and it feels easy and right. Try to make sure you have it before the audition starts. Sometimes, and it's really frustrating, I'll find the hook *on the way home* from the audition. That's a bummer.

6. Getting ready routine

Now that the homework is done and it's time to get ready to go to the audition, you should begin your getting ready *routine*. Most performers, including athletes, usually have a routine or ritual they follow religiously when preparing for a performance or a game. It's a personal preparation schedule that allows the performer to peak at just the right time. In your case, it's when you walk into that audition room.

You will discover your ritual over time. After a few auditions, you should start to notice a routine and rhythm to your preparation. It is important to be conscious about it and not let other work, emergencies, and life throw you off schedule. If you are aware of your ritual, you'll be able to tell when you're off your pace, be able to adjust, and get back on track.

Start to notice what you do that helps, and what you do that gets in your way. Be conscious of how long you need to prepare for each audition, and routinely do what works for you.

Performers are fanatically superstitious about following their routines which can start a few minutes or a few hours before the performance. It is a physical and mental preparation time. For instance, most athletes always pack their gear in a precise order in their sports bags; they will show up to the locker room as close to the same time as possible before the game, and do the same warm-up routine they always do, with the intention of being physically ready and mentally focused when the game starts.

So for you, the actor, the preparation ritual might include:

- ➤ Physical and vocal warm up.
- ➤ Doing your hair/make-up, shaving, etc.
- ➤ Getting into your wardrobe.
- ➤ Doing a relaxation exercise or meditating.
- ➤ Listening to music that puts you in the appropriate mood.
- ➤ Going through the material one last time.
- ➤ Going over your checklist of what to bring.
- ➤ Getting to the audition 15 minutes or so early.
- ➤ ...and anything else that works for you.

Having a personal routine helps you to focus, concentrate, and be in the zone. Being conscious of your routine allows you to know if you're on schedule or not. You can adjust accordingly, and peak at the appropriate time – when you walk into the audition room.

7. **What to wear**

The most important elements of dressing for an audition:

-- You put your outfit together *in advance* so you're not scrambling at the last minute, trying things on and pulling clothes out of your laundry basket.

-- Your outfit gives a *suggestion* of how the character would dress. You don't need to rent a costume. If you are reading for a specific kind of uniformed role; such as a cop, a nun, a priest, or a doctor, you don't need to show up in full costume.
Just wear a style and colors that suggest that role. On the other hand, if you know you go out for lots of nurse or doctor roles, you might want to invest in a white lab coat; if you read for blue collar roles such as mechanics and truckers, you might want to have a pair of overalls in your wardrobe.

-- Your outfit *suits you*. If you were this person, how would you be dressed? Do not wear clothes that you would personally *never* wear; it's not that important. Remember, you've cast *yourself* in this role, so dress the way *you* would in this character's situation.

Give your wardrobe some thought. You want them to see you in this role, so how you look counts.   Clothing also changes how we feel, affects how we carry ourselves, and makes a statement about our personality. How you *feel* in the clothes matters a great deal, so pay particular attention to it. You need to feel as if you are the character, so make sure what you're wearing supports that; if it doesn't, change the outfit.

<u>NOTE TO WOMEN</u>: If your character could be in either pants or a skirt, go with the skirt. Showing off your figure never hurts. Sometimes they actually need to see what your shape looks like for a specific reason in the script.

<u>NOTE TO WOMEN AND MEN</u>: Unless you are reading for a grubby character, always be neat and tidy. You should have clothing that suits the roles you usually read for on stand-by – ready to go on short notice.

What to wear on camera:

- <u>Stay away from wild prints and narrow pin stripes.</u>
  They tend to jump and move on camera. It's distracting.
  You want the auditors watching you not your clothes.

- <u>Solid black makes your skin tone lighter.</u>
  The iris in the camera opens wider to let more light in so it
  makes everything lighter, including your skin.

- <u>Solid white makes your skin tone darker.</u>
  The iris in the camera closes to balance the brightness;
  it makes everything darker, even your skin.

What to wear on camera: (cont'd)

- <u>You can wear black and white combos.</u>
  The black and white together balance the light, so
  you can wear a combination of those.

- <u>The myth about the color red:</u>
  Because of the advanced technology of cameras these days,
  you *can* wear red.

Jewelry:

- Usually, less is more for auditions. Unless the character requires lots of bling, keep it simple.
- Just as for clothing, what would you wear if you were this character? If the character wouldn't wear jewelry, remember to take yours off.

Makeup and hair:

- Normal street/daytime makeup is best.

- If the role requires less make-up or more than you usually wear, do what's appropriate for the role.

- The same rules apply to hair – be appropriate for the character.

- NEVER LET YOUR HAIR FALL INTO YOUR EYES OR FACE! This applies to you men as well. They want to see your eyes.

- <u>Men:</u> You have it easier than the women, but you should put some thought into whether to shave or not, and keep that hair out of your eyes.

8. What to bring

Before you leave for the audition, check and make sure you've got everything you need with you. Here's a basic check list:

- ☐ **Photo & resume** – Even if you know they have one, sometimes they want another one.

- ☐ **Sides** – The ones that you used for homework. You may want to look at your notes, even though they usually have sides there.

- ☐ **Location info** – Particularly if you haven't been there before.

- ☐ **Props** – If you plan on using something, bring it. They may not have what you need there.

- ☐ **Personal info** – For the Contact Sheet you will fill out when you get there. You'll need your contact address and phone; agent's phone, and if you have one your company name, ID# and tax code, your SIN or SSN, your measurements and clothing sizes, and your Union #'s (if applicable).

- ☐ **Water** – They may or may not supply it and you want some in case of dry mouth.

- ☐ **Change for parking or public transit** – You want to be sure you're prepared so you're not panicking about stuff like that at the last minute.

- ☐ **Cell phone** – In case you run into traffic or trouble and are going to be late, you can call your agent or the casting director. Remember to turn it off when you arrive.

9. Focus on task

Give yourself ample time to focus on getting ready on audition day. If at all possible stay calm. Don't have anything else going on so you can prepare at a comfortable pace with no other distractions.

That means *no phone calls*! Don't make calls or answer your phone. Let whomever is calling leave a message and deal with it after your audition. Save those calls you have to make until after the audition.

Don't run errands, or think about things you need to do at least a couple of hours *before* you start preparing. There will be plenty of time *after* to deal with the rest of your life. It's important that you keep yourself in the character's frame of mind. Put your energy and concentration on one thing – the audition. Stay relaxed, do whatever warm-up you need to do. Get yourself into the role and stay there until the audition is over. You don't need the baggage of your own life right now; if you let it in, there's a good chance that it could affect your audition in a negative way. If your baggage is similar to the characters then use it; otherwise, put it on hold. Your life will be waiting for you when you finish.

I heard a story from a director about wanting to cast an actress whom he knew was perfect for the part – only to have her come in and blow the audition for the producer. The director asked her what had happened. She said that just before she left the house, her mother called and they had a fight on the phone. Well, the director couldn't go back and give the producer that excuse, so she was out of luck.

If you are too sick or upset to do your best, *cancel and try to re-book*, or try to get in on call backs. *Never* go into an audition with excuses why you're not your best today. The truth is they don't care, and it looks like you're covering your ass in case you fail. If you are sick or upset, go anyway, *get over it* for the few minutes you're in the room and don't mention it. The adrenaline rush will make you feel better when you're done.

10. Leave early

Make sure you give yourself ample time to get to the audition. You need time to deal with traffic or transit delays, find parking, find the address, and still be there early enough to calm yourself and re-focus on the material before you have to go into the audition.

BE AWARE AND BEWARE:

The *good* news may be that you have two auditions almost back to back: the *bad* news is that you have two auditions back to back! Here's how to handle this situation:

- ✓ Do your performance prep for both in advance.

- ✓ Make sure your agent has spaced the times far enough apart so that if the first one runs late (as they tend do) you're not in a panic. Make sure you have enough time to travel, possibly change wardrobe, and re-focus.

- ✓ On the day of the auditions, focus on audition #1 until it is over. As soon as it's done, let it go and focus on audition #2.

- ✓ If it looks like you'll be late for audition #2, have your agent notify the casting director. Then you can relax and get into Audition #2 in a calm state, not in a panic.

ALWAYS CALL AHEAD:

Don't be late. But if you are going to be late for whatever reason, always call ahead. First of all, it's common courtesy. It's how professionals behave. Secondly, even if they are behind, casting directors *do notice* if you're not there. Don't assume they are always behind. The day you do that, they will be on time. Thirdly, it will relieve the stress and pressure of feeling guilty and worrying about being late and will help you stay calm and focused on the task at hand.

CHAPTER TWO

THE AUDITION

1. Who might be there

Before I take you into the room, here is some information about who might be there and how much weight their votes carry. But when they are in the room consider everyone to be of equal importance.

Network/Studio Reps are usually not there in the first or second round of auditions. In fact, you may never meet them; but they might show up for callbacks. Most of the time, they won't say much. They let the Producer and Director run the session, but they have final approval of the cast. For lead and supporting roles in TV series and Feature Films, you may have to go to the Network/Studio – meaning you will have a final audition for them. At this point there may be two or three actors in the running for the role.

Producers narrow the field of choices and may have final approval of the casting if they also represent the Network/Studio, or if they are independently producing the project. There may be more than one of them in the room, or none of them may be at the first audition.

The Director will be allowed a strong opinion and vote, but unless his contract includes final cast approval he will not have final say in the matter. He/she will also contribute to narrowing the field of choices for the roles. He/she might not be there for the first round of auditions either.

NOTE: The Producer/Director relationship will determine how much weight the Director's vote carries. If the project is an episode of a series, it's usually the Producer's final choice. For features, it may be that the Director's vote counts as much, if not more, than the Producer's vote.

The Casting Director is usually in the room and may be your reader as well. He/she may or may not be allowed an opinion, and may or may not have a vote. Their job is pretty well done once you're in the room. The only thing they have left to do is book (make the calls and do the paperwork) the actors that the producers and directors choose. Occasionally, they may have the opportunity to recommend actors, or cast some of the very small roles with their own choice.

The Camera Operator will probably be obscured by the camera, but he/she is a participant in the process. It's wise to include them in your greeting. They are the ones who are responsible for how your audition looks on camera. You want them to be *conscious* of what they are doing and you want them to be on your side. When I acknowledge this person it reminds me that the camera is part of *my* process as well.

The Reader (if it's not the Casting Director). Some casting directors hire readers (usually actors) to read with everyone who comes in. It's *especially important* to connect to this person since you'll be doing the scene with them.

Miscellaneous others. There might be a few others in the room who are connected to the production in some way. It could be the Writer, the Director of Photography, even occasionally family and friends of the Producer or Director.

> NOTE: It's really important to be *listening* when people are introduced, not so much to remember their names, but to know their position with this project. Whether they are introduced or not treat everyone with the same amount of respect. You never know who's who; it could be that the little old lady in the back of the room who looks like a friend of the family might actually be the Producer or Network Rep., and the guy in the suit who looks like a Producer is one of their cousins just tagging along.

2. Types of auditions

Basically, there are *four* types of auditions. You will be required to do only one or two of these, depending on the project or you might have to go through all of them for just one job.

1. The Pre-screen

You might have to start at this level, particularly if you are meeting a casting director for the first time. Because they don't know your work, or character type, you may have to audition for them before they bring you in to tape or read for the Producer/Director.

These auditions are not usually on-camera and the Casting Director will probably read with you. If he/she thinks you should audition for the role, you will be invited back for Audition #1.

If this is a live (no camera) audition, you don't need to think about camera logistics; just connect to the reader and play the scene. You might be asked to sit and read the scene with them. If it is on-camera for some reason, then all of the audition rules apply.

If you've done a good job and don't get invited back for Audition #1, don't feel badly. Unless your agent gets negative feedback you did a good job. The Casting Director just didn't think you were the right type for the role.

It's a good idea to have your agent ask for feedback since it was your first audition with this Casting Director. Your agent should be curious about how it went anyway.

If the Casting Director liked what you did, he/she will see you for other things. It's at least a foot in the door even if you didn't make it to the next level.
If you didn't do a good job the Casting Director may not want to see you again for a long time, so it's pretty important to do your best at these.

2. **Audition #1**

You may be called to Audition #1 with or without the pre-screen. This is the first on-camera taping, and might be one of the following:

Just tape session: there will only be the Casting Director, reader, and camera operator present. The major players will look at the tape later and either hire directly from this tape, or select the people they would like to meet in a call back audition. I consider this a form of pre-screen since the people who have the final say aren't there to meet me, but it is often a necessary step to get to this next one:

Producer/Director session: The session will still be taped and even possibly streamed to other monitors, and the Producer and/or Director will be in the room. I prefer this kind of session as a first audition. I love the live audience and I might get some tips from them on what they're looking for.
The director may even work with you in this session. If he/she does, don't panic. It doesn't mean you're not doing well; it means they are interested in you. If the Producer and Director are there, there's a good chance they will hire from this session, but there might be a call-back.

3. **The Call-Back**

You've read at least once and they want you to come back again to meet you for the first time, to have you meet some other people, and/or to see everyone again now that they've narrowed down the field. There may also be a few actors there who are reading for the first time. Maybe they couldn't make the first audition, or the Producers needed to see more people.

Always go to the call back dressed exactly the way you looked at the first audition, unless you receive other instructions.

Call-backs should not make you more nervous even though you may feel more pressure. They are calling you back because they like what you did and how you look; so unless you get other directions, do exactly what you did the first time. If they want something different, they'll let you know.

If they are having trouble deciding who to cast or they need Network approval, you might be asked back for a *second* call back, or even a *third*. Each time the field of potential choices will probably narrow. It could be that there is a power struggle going on if it's a decision by committee. In this case, there may be an actor or two auditioning for the first time, even at the second or third call-back. No matter what you think is happening try to let each call-back make you calmer, though that can be tough. Don't let the pressure get to you. Concentrate on the fact that they love you. Help them see that you would be the best choice by staying strong, relaxed and focused in the work.

4. The Screen Test

This is about as nerve-racking as any audition could be. If you're up for a regular role on a series or a lead in a major feature film, you may have to go through this process. They may be "testing" a couple of actors for the role, but the field has been narrowed down to just these two, possibly three.

This audition is the full-meal deal; your hair, makeup, and maybe even your wardrobe will be done for you. Your reader will be another actor who's been cast in a role, an actor who is hired just to read, or possibly the director. It's filmed on a sound stage with the proper equipment, props, furniture (to a degree), etc. The director and/or producer may or may not be present. If they are, they may give you directions. You will probably get a rehearsal for camera. You may or may not get to rehearse any more than that, or even get a second take.

This audition will certainly test your ability to stay relaxed and calm, be in control and get the job done. Focus your attention on the scene – forget everything else once that camera rolls. Don't forget to breathe!

SPECIAL NOTE: Some directors hate the audition process. Occasionally (but rarely), directors (usually European) may not have you read. They may just have a chat with you to experience your essence and your personality. They may talk with you about the character, your life, or life in general, and/or have you do a very casual reading of a scene. They decide if you suit the role from their experience of who you are.

They've seen your resume and trust that you are being recommended because you know how to act. They are also confident that they know how to direct an actor to give them what they are looking for. They only need to meet you and get a sense of who you are in order to know if they can work with you. So enjoy not having to read and be genuine.

CHAPTER THREE

HURRY UP AND WAIT

1. Getting there

You should be at the audition *before* your appointment time. Whether it's half an hour, 15 minutes or 5 minutes, depending on what works for you, be there early.

CAUTION!

Once you are in the vicinity of the audition, especially when you get to the building, put on your friendly face and positive attitude. Sometimes the very people you will be auditioning for are around that area, but you won't know who they are until you get into the room.

Be careful about your conversations with other actors as well. You don't know who may be listening.

I've heard stories about actors behaving rudely, or conversing with another actor about the bad script, only to find out that the person they were rude to or who overheard the conversation was actually the producer.

Following are some tips on what to do and what not to do when you get there:

...hurry up...

...and get the following done...

1. Check in: There is usually someone at the front desk you should check in with, or wait until the casting director comes out, then let them know you are there.

2. Sign in: There will usually be a Sign-In Sheet in the waiting area. The example I've included here is for a union audition, but there is usually a similar one for non-union as well.

APPENDIX "G"

AUDITION SIGN-IN SHEET

Page _____ of _____

Production Name: _____ Audition Date: _____

Casting Director: _____ Casting Assistant: _____

Episode # _____ of _____

Call Time = Time audition is scheduled to start / Arrival Time = Time performer arrived at audition / Time at end of audition = time performer is released

PERFORMER'S NAME ☆PLEASE PRINT CLEARLY☆	UBCP MEMBER #	R O L E	CALL TIME	ARRIVAL TIME	TIME AT END OF AUDITION	PERFORMER SIGNATURE (Sign only upon completion of Audition)	PLEASE CHECK ONE ☑ :		
							Canadian Citizen or Landed Immigrant	U.S. Citizen living in Canada w/ Visitor Status	U.S. Citizen living in the U.S. / Other:

UBCP
UNION OF B.C. PERFORMERS
B.C. Branch of ACTRA

300-856 HOMER ST., VANCOUVER, BC V6B 2W5 • PHONE: (604) 689-0727 • FAX: (604) 689-1145

APPENDIX "G"

SIGN-IN SHEET

3. Fill out paperwork: There might also be an Information Sheet to fill out. This one is for your personal contact information, agent info, sizes and availability for shoot dates, etc. Fill this out and turn in all paperwork along with your picture and resume. Here is a sample of what that sheet may look like:

INFORMATION SHEET

Auditioning for the ROLE of:

NAME (as appears on credit):   _____

AGENT:_____   AGENCY:

AGENCY CONTACT #:   _____.
COMPANY NAME:
(Or if under 18 years, parent's name)

PERSONAL CONTACT #: _____(home)   _____(cell)

Email:
_____.

(Fill in ONLY if under 18 years of age)
DATE OF BIRTH & AGE:

SIN#: _____   GST#:

AFFLIATIONS:

UBCP#: _____   ACTRA#: _____

SIZES (where applicable):

Dress:_____   Pants:_____   Jacket:_____   Shirt:_____   Shoe:

Hat: _____   Bust/Chest: _____   Waist: _____   Hips:

Height: _____Weight:_____ Eye Colour:_____ Hair Colour:

AVAILABILITY:

Are you available on May 28th? (subject to change)

_____

4. <u>Do bathroom/mirror check:</u> Once you've done all of the above, find a mirror and do a final check of your appearance. Make sure your hair, makeup, and clothing are in order.

5. <u>Relax and focus on your material:</u> If you still have time, settle down and take a look at your scene. For some actors, pacing is a way of settling down; for others just sitting and relaxing is enough. Do what works for you.

<u>WARNING:</u>

If you arrive well before your call time and no one else is waiting to go in because they are actually ahead of schedule, DO NOT let the Casting Director take you into the audition *before you are ready.* If you are really ready, go ahead. If you're not settled, focused and prepared, no matter how insistent they get, *do not* give in. Stand your ground.

If they ask you to come in and you're not ready, tell them you are actually early and need a couple of minutes to settle down and focus. If they are pressuring you to hurry up, tell them you have to go to the bathroom; then go to the bathroom and don't come out until you *are* ready. It's not your fault they've gotten ahead of schedule, and your being ready is extremely important.

Of course, if you are just on time or late, you don't have a leg to stand on. You *must* go in, which is usually a disastrous situation. If you are early and you let them take you in before you're ready it will be a disaster as well and you'll have no one to blame but yourself.

I've heard more than one horror story from students who were afraid they would make the casting director angry and didn't listen to my warning. They let themselves go in before they were ready and blew the audition. They got really nervous, were distracted and completely out of control in the scene.

I've even done it myself before I got smart and took control of my own auditions. I've kicked myself all the way home, too!

...then wait...

...and do the following...

2. <u>What to do/what not to do</u>

It frequently happens that they are running behind. If you were early for your appointment, you have even longer to wait before your turn comes. If you've done all the paperwork, etc. and have nothing to do but wait, here are some tips about handling your time:

<u>Stay focused</u>: Stay private and focused on your material. As I've said, you can sit or pace but go over the lines and your choices, and don't chat with other actors. It's distracting to you and them.

<u>Use positive reinforcement</u>: Keep yourself in the proper emotional state and concentrate on what you *are* going to do:

    For example: If you're feeling nervous, tell yourself:
    -- I'm going to relax
    -- I'm going to breathe
    -- I'm going to channel the energy of how I'm feeling
       into how the character is feeling.
    -- I'm going to remember my lines.

<u>Don't use negatives.</u> Be conscious of negative thoughts. If you tell yourself what you're *not* going to do, you will reinforce those negatives and do exactly what you don't want to do:

    For example: If you're feeling nervous, *don't* tell yourself:
    -- I'm not going to be nervous.
    -- I'm not going to tense up.
    -- I'm not going to panic.
    -- I'm not going to forget my lines.

NOTE:

> Sometimes the waiting room gets crowded. If people are being noisy or the energy in the room is interfering with your concentration, take yourself as far away from it as you can. Just be within range of hearing your name called to be on deck, meaning you are next, or let the casting assistant know you're stepping out for a few minutes. Find out how many people are ahead of you and check back to see if it's getting close to your being on deck.

3. Nervous vs. Excited

Auditioning can be stressful. The *bad news* is that the nerves may never totally disappear no matter how many auditions you have done. The *good news* is that you will learn to live with those nerves and not let them affect your performance in a negative way.

I've done hundreds, maybe thousands, of auditions and still to this day, I might be calm or I might be shaking. Over time, I've learned to channel that nervous energy into the scene and turn it into the emotional or physical energy I need for the character. These days I shake more after the audition is over -- I think it's the adrenaline rush.

I've also learned that the physical symptoms of nervousness and excitement are exactly the same: butterflies in your stomach, shaky limbs, heart palpitations and sweaty palms.

Psychologically, how you let it affect you depends on what you *call* it.

Here's the difference:

If you call it *nerves* you'll be thinking:

> ➢ This must be bad...
>> ➢ Something is wrong...
>>> ➢ I should be worried...
>>>> ➢ There's something to fear...
>>>>> ➢ I don't want this to happen...

If you call it *excitement* you'll be thinking:

> ➢ This is a good thing...
>> ➢ I'm glad this happening...
>>> ➢ I'm looking forward to this...
>>>> ➢ There's nothing to fear...
>>>>> ➢ My energy is flowing...
>>>>>> ➢ I can hardly contain myself...

In either case, it's just energy, with probably a good dose of adrenaline flowing through you. So use it to your advantage. Don't try to resist it. Accept the symptoms and see how you can use them in the scene:

- ✓ Is my character excited?
- ✓ Is my character nervous, angry, unsure, etc.?
- ✓ Use the heightened awareness the energy brings,
  even if your character needs to be calm and in control.

CHAPTER FOUR

FINAL PREPARATION

1. <u>Affirmations</u>

If you've covered everything you need to do before going in and you're still waiting, spend the rest of the time thinking about positive possibilities that await you. You need to want to be in that room.

Do some affirmations about being in the room. Think about all the good things. For instance:

> -- I'll meet new people who are warm and friendly.
> -- I will have fun and *knock their socks off*.
> -- They will love what I'm going to do with the scene.
> -- If not this role, they will find another role for me.
> -- They will remember me for their next project.
> -- The casting director will be pleased and see me again.

...and anything else you can think of...

2. <u>Gratitude</u>

If you're still a little unsettled or feel nervous, think of things you are grateful for. It doesn't matter how big or small. For instance:

> -- I found a great parking space.
> -- I can pay my bills. I have food and shelter.
> -- I've been working hard on my craft and I'm prepared for this.
> -- I'm grateful for this opportunity.
> -- I'm grateful for the people in my life.

...and anything else you can think of...

Remember, it's what you are there *to give,* not what you're there *to get.* So far, from preparation to getting there it's been all about you; now you can think about what you would like *to do* for them. It will get your attention off yourself.

For instance:

    -- I want to give them a break from this tedious casting session
      and give them a few minutes of pure entertainment.
    -- I want to send them energy, blessings, love.
    -- I want to make them laugh, lighten up, have fun.
    -- What do I want to leave them with?

3. **You're "on deck"**

On deck means that you will be next and the casting director or assistant will let you know that. When you are on deck, you should get up and move around a bit; make sure your energy is flowing.

It's going to be your turn in just a few minutes. All you can do at this point is to take some deep breaths, calm yourself, and focus on this moment. Don't let your mind run away on you now.

If the reader comes to get you, look over the sides with him/her. Make sure you have the same pages, co-ordinate your start and stop places in the scene/scenes. If not, check with the reader when you get into the room. When you go in...

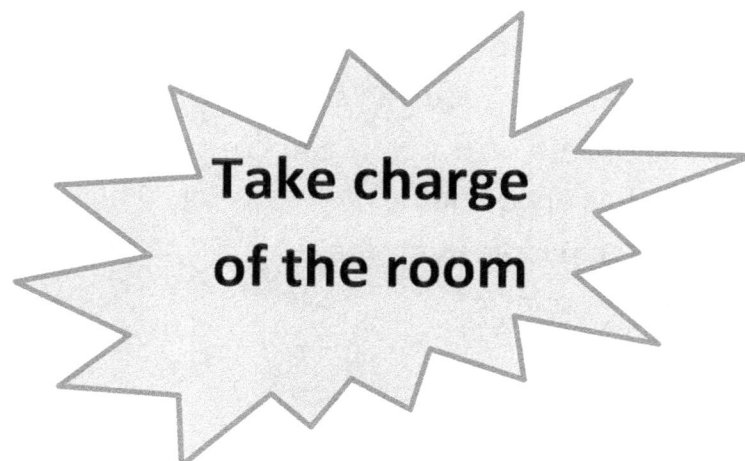

**Take charge
of the room**

CHAPTER FIVE

YOU'RE IN THE ROOM

1. The interview

When you step into the room, take a breath, be in the moment and focus on seeing:

✓ See the room
  ✓ See the camera
    ✓ See your mark, head in that direction
      ✓ See who else is there
        ✓ Be aware of the vibe in the room
          ✓ Make eye contact with everyone
            ✓ Say "hello"
              ✓ Settle yourself down

DO NOT shake hands unless someone offers theirs first.

If the Casting Director introduces everyone, really try to hear their names and titles. Make eye contact with each one as they are introduced. You probably won't remember their names, but the connection is important. What keeps you scared is who you *imagine* is there. The *reality* of who is there will calm you down and dispel the perception that they are monsters and are out to get you.

When you actually connect with them, you might see people who seem to be in worse shape than you are, or you see friendly faces. Every now and then you may see someone who looks unhappy but that's not because of you. He/she is having a bad day. Don't' let that throw you.

I've gone into sessions and thought that the producers and directors were looking a little rough around the edges; either they had been sitting in one spot for hours or there was no air left in the room. I usually offer to wait while they take a break, walk around, open a window and get something to drink, or turn on the air conditioning. My offer has always been met with appreciation, if not action, and I always wonder if my attention to their well-being had something to do with my booking the job. Regardless, I know it can't hurt.

If the Casting Director, Producer or Director initiates a conversation, then have a chat; otherwise, follow the CD's lead. They may ask if you have any questions (about the scene). If you have one ask, but don't make something up just to talk. If they don't ask and you have a question, now would be a good time to say so.

They may or may not chat, but if they do, be prepared to be asked about the very thing you don't want to talk about. I'm not sure how they know but they usually can hit the mark:
-- If you have an issue about your age, they will ask how old you are.
-- If they look at your resume, they will pick the production that was the worst experience of your life and ask how you liked working on that show.

<u>On lying:</u>

My rule is that it's is okay to lie *as long as you don't mind getting caught*. For instance, some actors put shows they weren't in to beef up their resumes. If you did that and got caught by a director would you dissolve in tears? Or would you keep your sense of humor and tell him you should have been in it but they wouldn't see you. If you would be crushed getting caught in a lie, don't do it. If you don't mind getting caught, then go ahead.

2. <u>Take charge of the room</u>

Once the interview is over and it's time to go to work, take charge of the room:
    ✓ Get set up and make sure you have what you need.
    ✓ Make sure things are where you want them: props, chair, water, etc.
    ✓ Settle into your emotional life.
    ✓ Now focus only on the scene.
    ✓ Do all of the above quickly.
    ✓ Indicate that you're ready, and...

3. Ready, Set, Go...

You may or may not be asked to slate your name. If so, do it when they roll camera and then go into your scene:

- ✓ Start with your *moment before*.
- ✓ Connect to the reader; *listen* to what he/she says in the scene.
- ✓ Trust that your choices are there, don't push; just *listen!*
- ✓ Finish with your *moment after*.

4. Finish

When the scene is over *say nothing.* Look to whoever is in charge for instructions and keep your mouth shut. If you start talking you're in danger of commenting on your work, or just babbling from the adrenaline flowing through you. At this point there are a few ways things might go:

They ask you to do the scene again with (or without) new direction or adjustments:
Great! You get a second kick at the can. If you get direction, make sure you understand what they want. Just *intend* giving it to them; don't work too hard to make sure that they see the adjustment.

They say, "That was great, thank you for coming":
If you feel you did your best then thank them and leave. Don't start a conversation or try to explain why you did it the way you did to illicit specific feedback.

They say, "Thank you":
If you feel that you could do better, instead of begging for a second chance say, "How was that for you? Would you like me to do something more... better... different?" Sometimes if you put the ball in their court, it opens a dialogue about what you did. You might get another chance, and it looks like it came from them.

CAUTION! If you get another chance, you had better be *better* than you were the first time. If they insist that the first time was great – you can only believe them and go.

CHAPTER SIX

WHAT TO DO WHEN IT'S OVER

1. On leaving...

On your way out, remember to thank whoever is there, including the cameraman and reader. Remember to sign out, and take a few seconds to gather yourself. If the scene was emotionally intense, you might need to recover in the waiting room for a few minutes. As soon as you're up to it, leave. Get out as quickly and as quietly as you can; don't disturb anyone else waiting to go in.

Don't hang around hoping they might want to see you again. If they do, there's nothing more fun than having them run after you to bring you back in. If they miss you, they know how to find you.

2. Reward yourself!

After you've worked so hard preparing and doing this audition, overcame all obstacles and survived this ordeal, I say you deserve a treat! You should reward yourself regardless of how you feel it went. It can be a small thing -- you don't have to buy yourself a new car. Go for a coffee, get a treat, take a cab home, or take an hour to do anything you want to do just for fun.

It may sound silly, but there are some useful purposes to my suggestion:

It may be the only reward you get. If you don't book the job, you at least get a treat; if you do book it, *double bonus*.

You will be more willing to move on. If there's a treat at the end of it all, you have something to look forward to no matter how the audition goes.

It helps you get your mind off the audition. Because it's something you're interested in having or doing, it can help distract you from thinking about how the audition went and wishing you could change it all.

3. Let it go!

This may be the hardest part of the audition process. You won't be able to get it off your mind easily, particularly if you don't think it went very well.

You might spend hours, maybe days: re-hashing what happened, wishing you could go back and change it, thinking about *if I'd only...* and *what if...*, waiting for feedback, hoping against hope that you might get it, waiting for that phone call.

There's nothing you can do about it now. The best thing you can do for your own sanity is to *let it go*. It's such a waste spending time and energy on it when that will have no effect on the ultimate outcome. Of course you need to allow yourself some time to process your feelings, but you need to get over it as soon as possible.

I'm speaking from my own experience. It will always take a little time to let it go, but you can consciously work on shortening the amount of time you spend on it. I did it for myself with my *reward* method and getting involved with my other tasks as quickly as possible. I got the time down to a couple of hours first and gradually worked it to somewhere between 10 to 15 minutes. It might take a few years and hundreds of auditions for you to get there, but it is possible.

It's still frustrating when I'm not sure how I did, or I think I didn't do very well. I keep running the scene in my head over and over, trying to fix it. Of course I can't, so then I'm waiting anxiously for some positive feedback to make me feel better. Thank goodness it doesn't last very long any more.

When I've felt really good about the work I've done in an audition, I've been able to let it go faster; it doesn't stick with me for long at all. There's something about knowing deep down that I could not have done *one thing* better. Whether they hire me or not, I am complete with the whole experience and don't need their approval to feel successful. It feels really good to be in that position!

4. Feedback

It's not always possible to get feedback on every audition you do. Casting directors don't have the time to give feedback on all the actors they see for each project. My motto is, no news is good news.

They do seem to find the time for feedback if they have an issue what you did; you will usually hear about that from your agent. If you don't hear anything at all, assume you did well – you just didn't book it.

As I've mentioned before, if it was a *pre-screen* or *audition #1*, it may be easier for your agent to get some feedback for you. Since it was your first audition with that casting director, your agent should also be curious and try a little harder to find out how you did.

I'm actually not a fan of feedback. I like the no news is good news rule. If you do get feedback, please take whatever it is with a grain of salt. Remember, art is a subjective experience; what one person didn't like about what you did, another person might love.

You may understand and agree with the feedback you get; in that case, make note of it for next time. If you don't understand or disagree with it, then don't do anything. Don't make major adjustments in your work based on the opinion of one casting director. If you begin hearing the same feedback from two or more casting directors, then where there's smoke there's probably fire and you should make some correction in that area.

If the feedback is all good, excellent! Congratulations! Keep doing what you're doing. You'll book something eventually even if you didn't get this job.

CAUTION !!!

Not all casting directors, producers & directors understand the acting process. They usually comment on the result they see; but what they notice may be a *symptom* of a different problem in your work. When you get this kind of feedback you might try to fix the *symptom* without addressing the underlying problem.

For example: A new student will come to me and their work looks *flat* -- I can barely hear them and they're just standing there. I'm not getting what's going on in the scene, so I ask why they're playing it that way. The answer is always the same, "I was told I was *too big* so I'm trying to be *smaller*." In this case they are trying to fix the *symptom*, not the real issue.

The issue is that the actor wasn't being *real*; the actor was *doing* the character instead of *being* the character. Or the actor is trained for stage, is used to playing to a big house and continues to do so for camera. When an actor does that on film, it always gives the appearance of being *too big* – that's what the audience sees so that's what they comment on.

The actor then takes the feedback literally and tries to be *smaller*, instead of trying to be *real* or just *playing to the size room* for film.

Trying to make an adjustment based on feedback can be actually harmful to the actor; it results in the actor over-adjusting, trying to fix the wrong thing and getting stuck.

If you get negative feedback and you have a teacher and/or coach, run the feedback by one of them. He/she will probably be able to sort it out for you, help you identify the real issue and solve the problem.

Another example that comes up frequently: You've done your scene, they say it was fine and they don't give you any direction at all. You get feedback that you weren't angry enough, or you were too angry, or whatever they took issue with. It can be very frustrating because you know that had they given you the direction you could have easily made the adjustment. There's nothing you can do about this one; so just let it go.

Basically, with regard to feedback, if you know you prepared well just move on. If you *didn't* prepare well be specific about necessary corrections, get the lesson, and move on.

Section Three: The Reality of Auditioning

CHAPTER ONE

GETTING AN AGENT

1. It's a start

Unless you are an excellent self-promoter, have an aptitude for marketing yourself, and are organized, disciplined, fearless and driven – you need an agent to represent you as an actor. Some successful actors say you need an agent, a manager, and a publicist to really get anywhere, but when you're starting out an agent is good enough.

Finding an agent can be a daunting task and finding a good agent who is the right fit for you can take a long time. If you're lucky you'll hit the right one quickly; otherwise, you might have to start with one who's willing to work with you. But if they aren't as perfect as you thought they would be, move on. I suggest you try the relationship for at least six months to a year. It will take time to know whether or not the partnership is producing satisfactory results.

If it's working for both of you that's great! If it's not working for either one or both of you, there is no shame in moving on. Actors change agents all the time. It can take years of exploration and experience to find the right fit. Some actors change agents because they feel their career is stagnant and they need to shake things up. Some agents might find it difficult to represent you well and decide to end the relationship. If that happens, don't be discouraged. Find a new partner to take you further in your career.

The most important thing to know regarding agents is that *you are hiring them*. They are not hiring you. You are paying them. They take a commission from what *you* make and, even though the checks may come through their offices, it isn't their money.

If they believe in your ability, they are willing to do the groundwork for free hoping it will pay off in the future, so you need to look at it as a *partnership* -- partners with expertise in different areas, working on your professional career. An agent handles the business side of things: getting you in to see Casting Directors, negotiating deals, signing contracts, handling payment, etc.; while you handle learning your craft and staying in shape, auditioning, staying up-to-date with all the tools you need (headshot, resume, etc.), self-promoting and supporting your agent in finding opportunities for you.

2. The tools

You will need the following tools for your agent search:

LIST OF AGENTS -- You will need a list of all agents in your area. The phone book or Internet will provide that information. Look for actor's information and Film Industry sites in your area. Lists are available through some local theatrical publications in cities where there is a large amount of industry activity. A theatrical bookstore can be another resource, or the library may have that information.

HEADSHOT -- If you have a headshot you've been using, keep using it; if you need one, get one done as inexpensively as possible. You don't need to get the most expensive headshots done by the best headshot photographer until you have found an agent. The agent may like you but not your photo; at that point, you can spend the big bucks and have really good ones done.

You really only need to send one pose, but if you have two send both. Keep your headshots up to date. Your photo needs to look like you, so don't have it touched up too much. Ladies, if you drastically change your hair style or color, you'll need a new photo. Gentlemen, if you sometimes sport a beard, you'll need a photo with a beard and one without. Just get the minimum number of copies to cover your submissions. It's better than being stuck with left-overs you may never use. If you are submitting on-line you will only need hard copies for the interviews.

<u>CAUTION</u>!   Headshots are different than portrait pictures and modeling portfolios. Make sure you have a photographer who knows what a headshot is. It should be a picture of how you really look (on a good day) and communicate the essence of your personality as well.

RESUME -- Regardless of how much or how little experience you have as an actor, you will need a resume to submit with your headshot. An actor's resume is quite different from a standard business CV.

In our business, training, skills, and hobbies count. Make sure you are clear about your level of expertise regarding athletic/performance skills and tell the truth about being a beginner, intermediate or advanced. You don't need to put your skill level on the resume unless you want to, but you might be asked about it. Some agents and casting directors don't want to see "extra" work on a resume as professional credits; I suggest you put it under *Training*. If you do a great deal of it, create a section called *Other Experience* and list the shows you've worked on.

Don't feel badly if you don't have a long list of professional credits. You have to start somewhere. Don't lie or make up credits unless you don't mind getting caught.

If you don't have enough to fill a page, you can always make the typeset a little larger.

Agents usually have a standard resume format for their clients. When you sign with an agent they will re-format yours to fit that standard and update it for you as your work experience grows.

See the example on the next page for a basic outline to follow in creating your own.

NAME

Contact info: (phone, e-mail)

HT:

WT:

HAIR:

EYES:

AGE RANGE: (5-8yrs.)

UNIONS: (if any)

FILM & TV

(show title)	(role: actor, principal,	(type, Prod Co, Dir.)
(name of project)	lead, guest star, etc.)	(ex: student film, VFF, name)
		(ex: MOW, NBC, name)

THEATRE

(show title)	(role: name of Character)	(name of theatre, Dir.)

TRAINING

(course, with whom, how long)

(course, with whom, how long)

SKILLS

(list in columns or straight line)

Ex: 1, 2, 3, 4, 5, 6...............etc.

Ex:	1	2	3
	4	5	6

NOTES:

- **EXTRA WORK can go under TRAINING, or be a separate category OTHER EXPERIENCE**

- **COMMERCIALS (if any) should be a line at the bottom of resume:**
  "LIST OF COMMERCIALS UPON REQUEST"

- **Skills & hobbies can include: driving standard, any athletics, other art forms,**
  Singing, dancing, dialects, instruments, etc...

COVER LETTER -- Whether you are submitting by e-mail or regular mail, you should include a *short* cover letter with your package by way of introducing yourself and stating your reason for contacting them. You can be creative with this and make it as personal an introduction as you like. Here are a few guidelines:

-- <u>Address the letter to a specific person</u> – Whenever possible, get the name of the agent you're submitting to and personalize it. Don't make it look like a form letter.

-- <u>If you have a name to drop</u> – Mention the name of the person who is referring you in the first line of your letter.

-- <u>Keep it short and to the point</u> – Do not tell them the story of your life.

-- <u>Stick to the facts</u> – Facts are interesting. Your beliefs and philosophies are not. A couple of specific facts about your career history should be enough.

-- <u>Don't state the obvious</u> – You don't need to tell them how sincere, dedicated, hard-working and passionate you are. They will assume this is true if you're pursuing this career.

-- <u>Be positive</u> – Express confidence that they will be interested and want to meet you; don't *hope* they will, or beg for an interview.

<u>Here's an example of one: (with a referral)</u>

> Dear (Agent Name),
> Linda Darlow suggested I contact you. I'm looking for representation
> as an actor here in (city). Attached is my photo and resume.
> I've recently relocated to (city) from (city) and am currently taking
> Audition Technique Classes with Linda. Although my background is Theatre,
> I'm very interested in making the transition to Film and TV.
> I've heard wonderful things about your Agency and am looking forward to
> meeting you at your convenience. I do have a demo tape I can e-mail
> to you upon your request.
> Thanks for your time. Looking forward to hearing from you soon!
> Sincerely,

<u>Here's another example:</u> (cold contact, no referral)

> Dear (Agent's name):
> I am currently seeking representation as an actor. Enclosed is my
> photo and resume.
> I've recently graduated from (school) and was heavily involved in
> the theatre department there. I've also been working on student films
> and independent projects over the past few years. It's time for me
> to start working professionally!
> I look forward to hearing from you and meeting with you at your earliest
> convenience. I am in the process of making my demo tape and will be
> happy to forward it to you on completion.
> Thanks for your time!
> Sincerely,

NOTE: If you have a demo tape ready to go, the last paragraph of the letter should include that information. If you don't have a demo ready, or one in the works, don't mention it. But eventually someone will ask for one, so get on making yours as soon as you start contacting agents.

DEMO REELS -- You should have a sample of your work on a disc and/or available to e-mail.

If you have copies of film work you have done, you should take short excerpts from those and put together a demo. It can be a few really short pieces or a couple of longer scenes, as long as *you* are featured in the scene.

If you haven't done any professional work, you can make a demo of material that suits you. It should be two short scenes, or a scene and a monologue, and be no longer than two to three minutes. It should look like an audition, with just you on camera and a reader off camera.

The pieces you choose should be contrasting in tone and attitude. If one scene is serious, pick another that is lighter and make sure the characters suit your personality type. Don't choose a recognizable star role from a movie or TV show that is always identified with that star, as the viewers will be thinking about how the star played it.

Don't put scenes you've done in class on your demo unless they are lit well and the sound is really good. If the scene you want to use is the one you did in class, fine; but re-do it properly and make the best high quality recording possible.

The beauty of the demo is that you have control over what you're sending to someone. Work on it until you have a spectacular one that you're proud to send out which will get you that interview. You don't have to hire a film crew or go on location (unless you want to); you can use a blank wall to shoot against, as done in auditions. You don't need to dress the set either; just use whatever basic set and props you want, and dress appropriately for the characters.

3. Shop around

A critical mistake actors make is that they zero in on some of the biggest and best agencies they desperately want to be with and start contacting those agents too soon.

First of all, the biggest and best might not be the best for you if you are just starting out. Secondly, if you have little or no experience interviewing agents, you don't want to take the chance of blowing it because you don't know how to handle the interview.

I recommend that you start by contacting agencies you *don't really want to be with* and practice your interviewing skills. When you don't care whether they take you on or not, there will be less pressure on you; you'll perform better and gain valuable experience. If they do want to take you on, you do not have to sign right away; you can tell them that you're shopping around and will get back to them when you've made a decision.

If you find another agent you would rather be with, go with that one; but make sure you let the other agency know. At the end of your agent hunt, if your first offer is still your only option, you at least have someone who will take you; someone is better than no one.

Most actors don't really enjoy the agent hunt. They want it to be over as quickly as possible, so they sign with the first agent who says, "I'll take you on". I suggest you shop around; try to see at least a few agents before making this important decision.

You should know what type of agent you're looking for and how you can best support each other in moving forward. Here are a few questions you need to ask yourself, so that you are clearer about what kind of representation would work best for you:

- ☐ Do I need lots of care and attention?
- ☐ Do I need to be in constant contact?
- ☐ Do I need my agent to be a friend and hang out together?
- ☐ Is it okay if I only hear from them when there's an audition or feedback?
- ☐ Do I want an agent who will be tough on me and keeps me on my toes?
- ☐ Do I need a business partner and a friend, or just a business partner?

See as many agents as you can. Get a feel for how they run their agency and find the best fit for you. Once you decide, you should give them at least six months to a year to see if the relationship is going to work. If it is, great; if it isn't, start the hunt again.

4. The interview

Remember that you are hiring them to be in partnership with you. You should be interviewing each other, so be prepared to *ask* questions as well as *answer* theirs. This meeting is not the same as an interview for a regular job; you should be relaxed and let your personality and energy come through. Dress neatly, but be comfortable and dress to suit your personality. Ladies and Gents, I hate to say this… but if you can look *hot* then dress *hot*; it counts in this business.

Even if you've sent them your pic and resume, take another along with you. In fact, if you have other head shots from your photo shoot, bring the contacts or discs as well; they may want to see other headshot options. Also bring your demo if they haven't seen yours yet.

Be prepared to have a chat about almost anything. Let them take the lead in the conversation; every agent has his/her own way of interviewing. Think before you speak; give specific information in your answers, and stick to the facts. Don't be afraid to stop talking; give them a chance to talk as well.

They will probably ask if you have any questions, so think about what you want to know. Here are a few things you might want to ask them about:
- [ ] How many actors do you represent?
- [ ] Do you have anyone like me on your roster and are they working?
- [ ] How do you prefer your actors to communicate with you?
- [ ] Do you have a good working relationship with the Casting Directors?
- [ ] Do you put actors on tape for projects outside of this area?

WARNING! If an agent says they will take you on *but only if* you study with a particular teacher, or take classes they offer, or go to a specific photographer -- be wary. They may be taking kick-backs or be running the agency solely on the income from their own classes. This usually indicates that they are not a strong agency in terms of getting their clients work. If they recommend a *few* teachers or photographers, that's okay. They are just suggesting options because they are interested in your development.

You may also be asked to do an audition. It may be material that they send you in advance, give you while you're there, or they may ask you to prepare something and come back. They should audition you for sure if they haven't seen your demo, but it might come up even if they have.

I wouldn't recommend signing with an agent who hasn't seen your work but wants to represent you. If they haven't seen what their clients can do, they may be sending weak actors on auditions; as a result, they probably don't have a very good reputation with the casting directors and aren't able to get many of their clients in to be seen. Make sure they are interested in seeing what you can do.

5. The decision

If an agent offers to sign you during your first interview with him/her, don't accept right away, even if you think this is the one for you. Thank him/her for the offer, say that you will get back to him/her, and *get out of the office*. Always take at least overnight to think about it. It's exciting to think your search is over and you've found someone who wants to work with you, but are you sure you want to work with them? Make your decision when you are calmer and not caught up in the heat of the moment. Give yourself time to think about it and live with it for a day or two before you make the commitment. If they want you today, they will want you tomorrow.

You might meet an agent who would be a perfect fit for you. They ask you to sign with them, but you've just *started* the search. I still recommend getting out of the office and taking time to make the decision before you accept the offer. If you still feel excited the day after the interview, and you are clear that this is the agent for you, I suggest you trust your instincts and go with them. You can either finish other interviews you've lined up and then let them know, or if you feel that strongly about them, cancel the other interviews. It happens.

If you've had a few offers to sign, be sure to let the other agents know you've chosen another agency and thank them for their interest. You might want to re-visit those agents if the one you sign with doesn't work out.

Finding the right agent for you can be a long and arduous task. It may take longer than you thought it would just to get in to see a few of them; but keep going and don't quit. You might sign with one who doesn't work out and it's back to the drawing board; that's okay too, just start the process all over again.

It helps a great deal if you keep an organized file on the agency contacts you have made.   It should include information on the agency name, address, phone number, your contact person, dates of mailings and phone calls, brief notes on feedback, and the ultimate resolution.

<u>For example:</u>

LD TALENT	Linda Darlow: 123-456-7890
750 Main – 2nd Fl.	
Vancouver, B.C. A2B 3C4	
1/20/2013 – E-mailed package	
2/15/2013 – Followed up with phone call, call back next week	
2/22/2013 – Not interested at this time, but okay to check again in six months	

Do a separate page or an index card for all of the agencies, and update as needed. When you are dealing with a few, it will help you remember exactly what has transpired with each one of them. You may think you'll remember what you've done, what each one has said, and when you should contact them again. You won't.

Not only will it help with your current search, but it will also be invaluable if you need to look for a new agent after a year or two.

GOOD LUCK WITH AGENT HUNTING!

CHAPTER TWO

STATISTICS AND ODDS

1. The facts

Just before I was leaving Los Angeles, back in 1985-86, I read a statistic published by Screen Actors Guild that made an impact on my perspective as an actor. I can't remember all of the details but the bottom line was that there were 200,000 actors in the union. 10% to 20% were working and more than likely it was the same actors doing all the work.

In 1995, in Vancouver, Canada, the Union of British Columbia Performers released performer earnings statistics showing that out of 1,254 performers 948 made *less* than $5,000 that year.

I wasn't able to update these statistics before printing, but my guess is that the odds have gotten only slightly better, if at all.

I'm giving you this information not to overwhelm or depress you (though it might), but to give you an overview of the reality of this professional acting business. You need to know what you're up against; you need to be aware of how many more actors there are than available roles.

Regardless of what the odds may be, you must believe that you can beat them; you must not let them get you down or stop you. You must have the courage and self-confidence to strive to be in that 10% to 20% of actors who *are* working. It should be a challenge you take on happily – against all odds.

Feeling defeated and hopeless about it will get in the way of your work. If you can't get past that information maybe this career isn't for you, but if you believe in yourself and are passionate about the process, then keep going.

There are well-known stories of famous actors who were told by industry professionals that they wouldn't make it. They succeeded because they believed in themselves, were determined to have a career in spite of negative feedback, and did it against all odds.

You should also be aware of how many actors actually get to audition for a role in Film or TV. Unlike commercials, when they usually see 50 to 100 actors per role, they usually see 6 to 12 actors for a Film or TV role. If they are having trouble finding the *right* actor they will see more, but the average number is 6 to 12. If they are on a worldwide talent search for an *unknown*, they might see hundreds to find that new young star; but that's an exception, not the rule. Lead roles in features and TV series, even some guest star roles, are usually cast from the producers and directors *wish lists* -- casting directors are given a list of actors to call in, or offers just go out to their first choice on the list.

Casting directors usually see the same actors over and over for the shows they are casting. They tend to see actors they know; actors with a track record, whom they know will make *them* look good. As a result, it may take some time for your agent to get you in to be seen by a major casting director; but with the right agent it should eventually happen.

I'm telling you this not to depress you but to have you understand that if you can even get an audition, you're already ahead of most actors. This is also why it becomes more important to do a great job when you have an audition since you are now one of the chosen few. You need to be as confident and secure as you can be to overcome the intense pressure and stress of finally getting a chance.

Your skills need to be in tip-top shape so that when you do get your chance, you can impress the casting director. Whether or not you book the job, it's more important that the casting director sees how good you are. Then you become one of the actors he/she sees all the time.

2. Who gets hired

My disclaimer in class: I can't teach you how to *book a job*. I can only teach you how to *do a good job* in the audition.

Having cast commercials and been through countless auditions myself, I've learned that it's not always the best audition or the actor's talent that wins the role. Casting is a subjective experience for producers and directors. There are also other factors that go into the decision-making process beyond how well an actor does in the audition:

-- Age. Do you look like the right age, regardless of your real age?

-- Physical qualities. Do you fit the producer's image of what this character should look like? Are there specific physical qualities required?

-- Personality. Is your personality the best fit for the character's personality?

-- Fit with other characters. Is your look and personality going to work best with the other actors they are casting?

-- Ability to take direction. Did you work fast and take direction well in the audition? Do they trust you'll be easy to work with on the shoot?

-- Track record. If you did well, but don't have many professional credits, they may decide to go with someone who has a longer resume. Usually, this depends on the degree of difficulty in the role.

-- Familiarity. They may decide to go with an actor they have worked with before rather than someone they don't know, regardless of how well anyone else did.

-- Local or import. If they are shooting the project on location in another city, do they want to cast this role locally or bring the actor in from another city?

-- Final approval. I've covered most of this in Section Two, Chapter 2, *Who might be there*. It's usually a decision by committee, but final cast approval depends on the type of project it is, who has contractual rights, and who has control of the money.

The committee is comprised of producers, directors, writers (sometimes) and casting directors (occasionally). The star of the show will have cast approval if it's in his/her contract; it doesn't happen often, but he/she might have a vote.

It has been known to happen that the committee members adamantly disagree on the choices, but a decision must be made. In order to settle the dispute, they actually agree to consider other actors who have not yet been seen and the job goes to one of those actors. The original final choices are out of the running. Fortunately, this does not happen often! You may have been one of the original choices and were told you were on hold, pinned, or even first choice; and then you don't get it and are left wondering what happened. If so, this could be the reason.

Ultimately, the Studio/Network has final approval (for series regular, recurring and guest star roles) in their Feature Films, TV Movies and TV Series. Supporting roles are usually cast by the producers and directors. In Independent Features the Executive Producer has final say.

SPECIAL NOTE: It has happened that an actor's audition is so strong that right or wrong for the part, producers and directors become attached. In some cases, they have actually changed the character's description to suit the actor and give him/her the role; or they've found another role for that actor because they had to have him/her in their show – another reason to do your best work!

EXTRA SPECIAL NOTE: If you appear confident, they have confidence in you. I also believe that the qualities of ease, openness, vulnerability, and being pleasant to work with, count as well. If you're comfortable with yourself, they will be comfortable with you.

3. <u>Your odds</u>

Given that there are so many variables in the casting/hiring process, it's almost impossible to book every audition you go on – no matter how well you do.

The best actor does not always get the job, and the strongest audition does not always win the role; but if you follow the *Four P's Rule*: passion, preparation, patience and persistence, your turn will come. I explain those in the next chapter.

In fact, I've come to believe there is such a thing as mathematical odds at play in an actor's career. If you track your auditions and keep a record of your own statistics, which you should, you will probably see a pattern unfold. Tracking your auditions includes:

-- <u>How many auditions?</u> Depending on the frequency, take an average of the weekly, monthly or yearly number of auditions.

-- <u>How many call backs?</u> Out of the number of auditions you are averaging.

-- <u>How many bookings?</u> Out of the same number you are averaging.

<u>Example</u>: You had 6 auditions in one month and 3 the following month; you had 2 call backs, and you booked 1 job. You have booked 1 out of 9 auditions. You then have 4 auditions over a two-month period, 1 call back and no bookings; but in the following month, you have 3 auditions, 2 call backs and 1 booking. You have booked 1 out of 7 auditions. So over 5 months, you've had 16 auditions and 2 bookings. Divide 2 into 16 and your odds are 1 booking in 8 auditions.

It might take you longer to have 8 auditions, which would result in it taking longer to book 1 job, but you can be fairly confident that after 8 auditions (however long that takes) you should be about to book one.

There is no rule. Each actor has his/her own odds and they're not good or bad. They are just the facts. One job for every 20 auditions can be good odds. One job out of even fewer auditions is excellent!

How often you audition will probably determine how often you work, depending on your odds. If someone seems to be booking all the time, they probably do even more auditions, and/or have better odds.

When I started keeping track, my odds turned out to be 1 job for every 10 auditions. Sometimes I would book more, sometimes less, within variable time frames; but the average remained the same. I found that very interesting.

It helps to know that every job I don't book gets me a step closer to getting one and keeps me looking forward to the next win, instead of being depressed about the losses. Somehow it makes rejection easier to take. Do the math!

4. Keeping a diary

You can easily track your odds if you keep an *Audition Diary*, which every actor should do. This is your business; you need to treat it as such, and keep detailed information on auditions, contacts, contracts, payments you're due, expenses, etc.

There are *Audition Diaries* in print or you can make up your own. Some are very fancy and expensive but some are basic and reasonably priced. If you're organized and like creating forms you can create your own and make it a fun project. You can keep it on your computer or make a hard-copy book.

It should include the following information: date of audition, name of project and type (FF,MOW, TV Series, Commercial, etc.), name of character you're reading for, production company info, director's name, location of audition, casting director info, what you wore, extra notes, and results (call back, booked, etc.). A separate page should include the other business information I mentioned above.

Following is an example of what one page of the diary might look like:

Audition Diary

Date: _____

Callback: __YES __NO

Booked it: __YES __NO

Project title: _____

__ Feature   __ TV Series   __ MOW   __ Indie   __ Student   __ Voice Over

__ Webisode   __ Commercial   __ Other _____

Production Company _____

Producer: _____

Director: _____

Casting Director: _____

Audition Location: _____

~~~~~~

Character: _____

What I wore: _____

How I think it went: _____

_____

_____

_____

_____

Feedback: _____

_____

_____

Notes: _____

_____

_____

Use any design you like as long as it has room for all the information you need. Make it fun to do; just because it's a business tool, it doesn't mean you can't have a good time with it.

Your audition diary will be useful for many things:

- Tracking your results and odds,
- Casting director/audition locations,
- Remembering directors you've read for
- Production company information and contacts,
- Remembering what you wore to first audition, should you get a call-back.
- Tracking which casting directors are seeing you and how often.
- Noticing the difference/similarity between how you thought it went and what the actual results were.

I love having my diary. It has become not only useful and informative, but also fun to look back on as a journal of my progress (or regression) in this profession.

CHAPTER THREE

PROCESS VS PRODUCT

1. Loving the process

In order to have a fulfilling career as an actor, you must love not only booking a job and creating the product, but also love the process of doing what it takes to get there. You are going to spend the majority of your time in the process and a minor amount of time creating product.

You should enjoy the entire process of being an actor with its ups and downs, highs and lows, stresses and insecurities. You also need to enjoy the hard work of it. The majority of your time will be spent studying, preparing, auditioning, and waiting to actually get a job. When you get the chance and have to deliver the product, a new set of challenges and stresses show up. Creating the product may take a day or two depending on the size role you've booked, while the *process* to get there may have taken a year or longer. When the job is finished it's time to start the process all over again.

I find the most fun time for me is between booking a role and having to do the role. The rest of the time it is just hard work; it's hard work getting a job and hard work doing the job. I happen to love the hard work. I love the process.

If you think that being an actor is an easy way to get rich and be famous, think again. There are much easier ways to make a good living. If you're in this business for the perks or the glamour talk to a successful actor. Occasionally there might be a glamorous moment or a few perks; the majority of the time, especially for stars, it will be long hours and exhausting work.

What if you spend years of your life in this business, hating the process and then you don't succeed? What then? Have you spent precious years making sacrifices, being unhappy and unfulfilled, with no product to show for it? Yes, you have. If you are happy, fulfilled, and consider yourself successful in the process, regardless of how much product you create, it doesn't matter if you make it, or not. You've spent those years doing what you love doing and you've survived. *Making it* is a relative term anyway; it depends on what you determine it to mean.

There is no guarantee that even if you achieve some level of success in this business it will be the status quo. Granted, if you establish a decent track record it may get a little easier to find opportunities, but there is never any real job security even if you book a regular role on a series that runs for seven years.

There's always a chance that the series will be cancelled, or that your character is eliminated from the story line. Having a role on a series, or doing a big feature film doesn't necessarily mean you'll get another one. That's why they say, "You're only as good as your last job".

If you love the process of being a performer, none of those things matter; regardless of the outcome, you are happy to be in the process and creating product whenever you get the chance. Maybe the *Four P's* will help you determine if you're suited to this process, then we can talk about creating product.

2. The "Four P's"

Passion, preparation, patience and persistence; if you can embrace these principles you will love the process of acting:

1) Passion – is the force that will drive you in your career.

If you're not passionate about acting you're probably not going to last long in this business. If you're not passionate find another career and be an actor as a hobby. If you can take it or leave it --then leave it, please.

If you're stricken with the acting disease and you're hopelessly addicted, then do it. "Disease" is actually a great word to associate with acting:

> "dis" – meaning away from…
> "ease" – meaning comfort, easy…

You have to be able to withstand a great deal of *dis-ease* as an actor:

> -- being rejected
> -- allowing yourself to be vulnerable
> -- being criticized while you're most vulnerable
> -- having no job security

If you are passionate about performing, it makes it much easier to put up with the *dis-ease*; so being passionate is one of the main requirements.

2) <u>Preparation</u> – is all about training, studying and being ready when the opportunities come along.

You need to keep your skills sharp and your instrument tuned up by working out on a regular basis. If you're not on a series or auditioning 2 or 3 times a week, even if you think you know everything there is to know about acting, you should be in a class; you need to practice to stay in shape.

I've had actors say, "No thanks, I've done my training". Well, in my opinion, you're never *done* training. There's always room for growth or at least the need for maintenance. If you were a dancer or musician you'd be practicing every day during your career; being an actor is no different.

I've also had actors say, "The business is slow so I'm not going to study now". It's when it *is slow* that you need to be working out regularly in class; so when auditions pick up, you are tuned up and ready to go.

I have actors come to me for coaching for an audition and I can tell they are rusty. I ask if they're in class – usually the answer is no. Well, the *one hour* that I have with them is just not enough time to get them back in shape after their *six months* of not working out. I think that is a shame. They now have an opportunity to shine and they're not up to it. You must get ready and then *stay ready!*

3) <u>Patience</u> – is a virtue you will need as an actor.

It can be a slow, long haul from...

    ...learning your craft...

        ...to getting an agent...

            ...to getting auditions...

                ...to working as a professional actor.

It can be very frustrating to work so hard learning your craft, investing a lot of money in training, working at jobs you don't like to pay for that training, and waiting for what seems like forever before you get any chances at all.

Understand that there are very few *overnight successes*. Accept that it might be a long haul. Have patience and enjoy being in the process. You will have a better perspective, a healthier attitude and probably more success.

4) <u>Persistence (perseverance)</u> -- is the staying power you need.

For a few, and I mean a few lucky or chosen ones, roles come quickly and easily. For the rest of us (the majority of actors) it takes time, energy and the ability to stick with it. It takes:

-- Looking for an agent *until* you find one.
-- Knocking on those casting director doors *until* they see you.
-- Feeling rejected over and over and *still being able* to audition
   enthusiastically for the next job.
-- Continually showing up *until* someone notices and gives you a chance.

Some actors put a time limit on their career goals. They'll say, "I'm giving it two years. If I'm not working by then, forget it". I say, why don't you forget it right now? This is someone who is only interested in the product, not the process.

Many actors average at least 10 years in this business before they even begin to get anywhere. *Overnight sensations* have usually been at it a lot longer than overnight -- it's just that no one noticed. Be persistent, passionate, persevere, and have patience; you will get your turn.

3. Creating product

"Stay conscious and self-generate"

-- Dan Fauci

Even though loving the process is all important, there *is* something extremely rewarding and fulfilling about creating a product. After all, it is our ultimate goal to produce *results*: a role, a job and a pay check, an acting career...

Getting that *big break* and establishing yourself as a professional actor is out of your control, but there are projects you can choose to do while you wait to become a star. They might not produce a big pay check, or any pay check for that matter, but they will give you some satisfaction in having created *results* and keep the flame of your passion burning brighter.

Do a play
You can take part in showcase productions and/or community theatre projects. You probably won't be paid, but you're creating a role in a production that will be seen; there's nothing quite like a live audience's acknowledgment of your work. You will be exercising your craft, and have an opportunity to network with others in the industry. You will also be making yourself visible and establishing yourself as a performer in the acting community.

Produce a play or create a one-man/one-woman show.
Make your own project. If there's a play you've always wanted to do, do it. Gather a group of like-minded associates and create a project for yourselves. If you have an idea for a show and you like to write, then write and perform it; collaborate with other colleagues and create a show. Having something clear and specific to work on will give you a sense of accomplishment with each step in the process. It can be scary, but less so if you surround yourself with support from others. It may be a long process, but it keeps you busy, creative, and involved while you wait for those other performance opportunities.

Do a Webisode

You can find one that is currently going on and get involved with it, or create your own. It helps to have a bit of a budget, but it can be inexpensive to produce with a small digital camera. It's a good film and TV showcase and it gives you visibility on a world-wide scale. More importantly, it can give you a sense of accomplishment in creating a product and producing results. I've seen a few that were terrific.

Be a reader in casting sessions

Some casting directors hire actors to read off-camera for those auditioning. This is an excellent opportunity, and may even pay you a few bucks; it helps if you are a good cold reader.

-- You get to practice your cold reading skills.

-- You watch other actors handle auditions and see what works and what doesn't.

-- If you are lucky enough to be a reader in a producer/director session, you will hear their comments; that experience should be an eye-opener for you.

-- Being a reader can actually lead to booking a role because the producer and/or director realize how good you are and find something for you in the project.

Look for work as a Stand-In

In film & TV they use actors to *stand in* for the principal actors while they set up lights and cameras. Usually you have to be close to the same height and coloring of the actor you're standing in for. You also have to watch the blocking and repeat the moves the actor will be making.

These stand-in positions actually pay pretty well; so well, in fact, that some performers wind up making a career of this job.

The other benefits include, being on the front line of the action on set; learning about how the set works; getting comfortable in front of the big cameras without the pressure of having to perform.

This work might lead to booking a role as well, particularly if you're a stand-in on a TV series. It's also a great way to network with cast and crew who work consistently in this industry.

Work as an extra

Although this is not as beneficial as other positions, it's a way of making money, as well as experiencing what it's like being on a set.

There is a myth floating around, that if you ever hope of being a principal actor you should never do extra work. *I disagree!*

The only extra work to avoid is what is known as "continuity extra" on a TV series; which means that you are established as a character who re-appears on the show, but never says anything. For example: the show takes place in a police precinct and you are usually present in the station as a background cop whenever they film on that set.

The down-side of continuity extra is that you won't be able to read for or play any other role on that show because you've been established as a character even though you don't talk.

The upside is that you have an on-going, paying job in the business. If they love you it could turn into a speaking role.

Otherwise, doing some one-shot extra work is fine. I don't think it gets in the way of your primary goal as an actor. To tell you the truth, they rarely notice the background actors, and if they do notice, it will probably be to your benefit.

I also hear actors say, "I don't do extra work because it'll hurt my career". My question is, "What career?" You can worry about that *after* you've established yourself. Even then, I see many *established, working* actors doing it just to pay the bills when the business is slow.

This takes me to the next level of creating product, and it deserves its own chapter on doing student films and independent projects. Read on...

CHAPTER FOUR

INDPENDENT and STUDENT FILMS

1. Student films

Many colleges and universities have substantial film departments; there are also a few stand-alone film schools. Usually, part of the curriculum includes making short films. If you are in an area near any of these schools it would be a good idea to check them out. These students are future main-stream film makers and they need actors in making their short films. Even if the school has an acting division, the students are allowed to go outside of the school to cast their projects.

You can go to the school's website for information or visit the school and check out their bulletin boards. Sometimes the school keeps files of photos and resumes for students to use when casting, and you can drop yours off to be put in their books. When they have projects coming up, they might post casting notices on websites that actors use for current film and TV information. They even post notices on Craig's List, Casting Workbook and Breakdown Services.

Students don't go through casting directors or agents unless they have a personal connection to them because there is little or no money to pay for their services. There's probably no money to pay the actors either so you won't make money; but you will gain experience – especially in the area of auditioning.

Yes, you will have to audition and this is the perfect arena in which to practice your skills. I can only simulate the atmosphere of an actual audition to a limited degree in my classes. Student film auditions take this to the next level.
They add the elements of:
-- auditioning for people you don't know.
-- competing for an actual role.
-- taking direction from student directors who may
   or may not know what they're doing.

-- experiencing what acceptance or rejection feels like
   even though it's a non-paying job.
-- feeling some of the stress and pressure of a real audition.
-- exercising your skills in preparation of new material.
-- networking -- meeting and working with future directors and producers.

These student films are the perfect places to practice your skills because:

-- It's a learning experience for everyone involved. Since everyone involved is learning, it's a pretty safe environment in which to test your skills, try things and develop your personal technique.

-- The auditions may be tougher than those for professional jobs. Because the students are new to the process themselves, they make up rather difficult tasks for the actors to do, make the audition space tricky to navigate in, or require the actor to execute more than is usually necessary in a professional audition.

-- If you blow it, the consequences are minimal. If you don't do well in this situation, it isn't going to affect your status with any major casting directors, or hurt your reputation as a professional actor. This is the perfect place to practice without jeopardizing your career.

-- If you book it, you get to practice your on-set skills. The actual shoot will be a learning experience for everyone so there's less pressure to get it right and you get some performance practice.

-- You can get a copy of the finished product. If you book it, you can get a copy of the short and use it on your demo reel if the quality is good.

-- It's a credit. You can use the credit on your resume.

NOTE: Because of everyone's lack of experience, student film shoots can be grueling. If you can survive these, you can survive any professional shoot.

2. Independent films

Independent means the project is not connected to a school, a TV network, or a film studio. It is a personal (or group) project that is being financed privately. There may be a small budget and these projects may not pay much, if anything, but again they are great projects to do.

On a larger budget independent, you could make a couple of hundred dollars a day. On a lower budget independent, you might be paid a small honorarium of $50/day or maybe $200 for the shoot. Some projects offer a deferred payment contract – which means if, and when, the project makes money you will be paid some kind of percentage or fee. It's usually a big "if"; so assume that deferred means you're doing it for free.

With the advent of HD cameras and the Internet outlet for projects, there are more and more independent film opportunities available. You might be contributing your time and energy, but it can be well worth it.

In addition to all the benefits of doing student films, independent films also tend to do the Film Festival circuits, looking for awards and distribution deals; more exposure for you, and who knows?... The project could find distribution and be the next big film event of the year.

If the producers have enough of a budget, they will go through casting directors and agents for their talent; but they may take the same route as student film makers, so check websites for casting information on these projects as well.

As with student films, these independent productions may be less experienced than major production companies; auditioning and working on the project can be more trying than working with the majors, but a valuable experience nonetheless.

The bad news might be that the project is quite disorganized, chaotic, and time consuming, as they try to figure it all out. Occasionally, the material is less than brilliant as well. Even going through the audition process can be weird and frustrating, so you may have to choose carefully whether to work on a project or not.

The good news is that since you're not very experienced either, you may be in good company. In fact, you may realize that you know more than they do and be able to help them out, so it's also excellent training for you. If you can survive these conditions, you can certainly do well in the big leagues with a team of highly experienced professionals.

I've always been open to working for little or no money and supporting up-coming independent film makers even though I have an extensive professional track record. It's an opportunity to give back to my community. I've also established wonderful relationships with some very talented new film makers who have given me the opportunity to do some character work that has allowed me to stretch as an actress. It's interesting that I have received more industry acknowledgment for *those* projects than for my mainstream work. I highly recommend always participating in both student films and independent projects, no matter what level of accomplishment you've reached.

Usually if you belong to a Union already these projects can apply for a waiver from your union which will allow you to work for little or no money on non-union or low budget productions.

3. Union or non-union

If you are new to this business then you're probably not a member of any Performers' Unions; eventually though, when you start working you will have to deal with them.

I'm not going to cover all of the specifics of joining a union here. That will be in my next book. I just want to say that there are pros and cons to being a union member. The most important of which is that once you are a union member, you cannot work on non-union projects, or you will face serious penalties imposed by the union.

If you are in any unions, you have a better chance of being seen for more mainstream projects and have the protection and benefits that unions provide. As I've said, being a union member does not prevent you from working on low-budget, indie or student projects, as long as the production applies to the union for a waiver on your behalf.

However, there is quite a bit of non-union work available if you're not in a union. Being non-union does not keep you from doing union work if they are willing to see non-union performers. The production may be allowed a certain number of non-union performers.

If you are non-union and book a union job, you become an apprentice with that credit. At some point, after accruing a certain number of credits, you will have to join the union as a full member.

Once that happens, you are no longer available for non-union work and there's a chance that the number of auditions you get will drop significantly, particularly in the area of commercials.

Unlike other unions, the actors' unions do not participate directly in getting their members work. It doesn't matter how long you've been a union member. Once you're in you're on equal footing with all other union members. I'm a member of six unions – SAG, AFTRA, Actor's Equity, ACTRA, UBCP and Canadian Actors' Equity – none of whom can get me a job.

They do look after contracts, residuals, rules & regulations for the production companies; they supply insurance benefits which are paid for by contributions from producers and from your fees. As you progress in your career, it is more beneficial to belong to the unions.

CHAPTER FIVE

EGO vs. SELF-ESTEEM

1. Believe in yourself

You have to believe in yourself as a performer. You can't rely on others, inside or outside of the industry, to generate that self-confidence for you. Actors often ask me if I think they have what it takes to make it in this business. There are two parts to my answer:

-- I don't know what it takes to make it.
There is no road map to success (at least that I know of) in this business. I might judge an actor's ability, but I've learned that my opinion about whether an actor can make it in this business or not is often wrong.

There have been many instances when I thought students or fellow actors were never going to make it, but they were the ones to land roles in TV Series or in Feature Films. There have been other students that I've thought were extremely talented and should have brilliant careers – they haven't.   I have never been able to figure out why that is, no matter how hard I've tried.

-- It's the wrong question to ask.
You need to ask yourself, "Do I have a burning desire to do this?" If the answer is yes, then go for it; stick with it as long as that desire burns. No one else knows the answer either, even though there are many who will tell you they do.

I've already mentioned those stories you may have heard about famous actors, stars, who were told they would never make it for whatever reason, but they did. They did because they believed in themselves and didn't listen to anyone else's opinion. Only you can know if you should be doing this or not. If the flame and passion die, then move on, if not, keep going. Believe in yourself and don't listen to anyone else.   Remember, it's the process that's most important; the product will be whatever it will be.

2. Ego

An ego is a good thing to have. The ego's job is *to serve and protect* us physically and mentally. Its job is to warn us of impending danger and keep us from harm; it's what keeps us from being hit by the bus. It's what identifies our individuality and helps us maintain our uniqueness; it's what allows us to say, "I am."

The problem with ego arises when it starts taking its job too seriously and perceives imaginary threats as real. It starts working overtime and goes on a power trip, causing you to over react when it feels threatened.

This business of acting is such a personal experience and requires such a deep level of vulnerability, that it can put your ego on alert, preparing to do battle, regardless of whether or not the threat is real.

I have a theory about stars throwing tantrums or making outrageous demands on set. I think it's just their egos raging out of control. It could be the ego over-compensating for a lack of self-esteem.

I also believe there are stars who are brilliant, work hard at what they do, and have earned the right to make some demands. Usually they are perfectionists who have such a strong work ethic they are given the reputation of being difficult when, in fact, they are only trying to make the best possible product.

I've worked with many stars who were supposed to be difficult and found them to be consummate professionals who have a low tolerance for mediocrity. Maybe I've been lucky in my career, but the majority of stars I've worked with have been easy-going, hard-working professionals; for the most part, they've been sincerely nice, warm, down-to-earth, and great team players.

There have been a few who seem to have little or no confidence and low self-esteem. Even though they have star status, acting is a difficult, almost painful process for them. They might cover this condition with what appears to be a huge ego, but is actually fear and a lack of self-worth.

Some actors who are new to the business think that if they have star quality they should have big egos. They make the mistake of allowing their egos to run amok, making them look rather foolish; they have no substantial experience, and no understanding of what the real ego issue is all about. In this day and age, there is little to no tolerance for this kind of behavior. It is certainly not what's expected of you and you won't get very far on that egotistical train; you can be replaced with an actor who is much easier to work with. I've seen it happen.

EGO...... is on the defensive

SELF-ESTEEM...... is on the offensive

3. Self-esteem

What you need in order to survive in this business is a healthy dose of self-esteem; you need an honest, positive evaluation of your self-worth, and it has to come from you. You must believe in your ability and talent. It may take time to develop this sense of self-worth, but training and experience will help give you that confidence.

Self-esteem, unlike ego, produces a quieter ease with oneself; it's a knowing, a comfortable security with one's ability, and a sense of worthiness.

Having self-esteem allows you to weather all the ups and downs you will experience as an actor; it allows you to maintain a healthy balance between the highs and lows in your career. It's what will give you the staying power for a long and fulfilling career, regardless of how far away or how close you come to realizing your ultimate goal.

4. Handling the lows & highs

Some of the highs and lows can be put in a better perspective if your self-esteem is intact. For instance:

Handling rejection:

As perceived through *ego*, rejection is taken as a painful judgment of your ability – you're not good enough. It can put a crack in your already fragile psyche; after being rejected as often as you will be in this business, you might have little or no belief in yourself left. It makes it very hard to go into the next audition with any confidence at all; you begin to face every opportunity with more dread than excitement.

There is a danger your insecurity will start to affect your work. Your ego, protecting you from further harm, shuts down your vulnerability instead of opening it up, and you feel stuck; then you over-compensate and push too hard in an effort to prove you are good enough. Instead, what you actually wind up doing is proving that you aren't good enough. Crazy, no?

~~~~~~~~~~~~~~~~~~~~~~

If it's perceived through self-esteem you see it differently. In fact, you don't perceive it as personal rejection; you look at it as an employer's subjective decision that has nothing to do with how you did – they just went with a different choice. You are able to accept that no news is good news; you can assume you did well if you don't get feedback. You understand that you will hear about it if you did badly. The casting director will probably call your agent who will in turn call you to find out what went wrong. It's understandable that you might be upset about not booking the job, but your thoughts and feelings are kept in proper perspective. It's about *not* getting a chance to do the role. It's *not* about being a bad actor.

This attitude allows you to face the next audition with enthusiasm and confidence no matter how many jobs you haven't booked.

Handling criticism from the ego's perspective:

An ego needing to defend your ability looks at criticism as a put down, a negative judgment, a black mark on your talent, a failing grade on your performance; something the ego can't allow. Remember, its job is to protect you from harm; sometimes you can't even hear the critique even though it may be valid, constructive and useful because your ego is blocking the *hurtful* information.

This can be a very dangerous particularly if your ego hears directions from a director as criticism. Your ego will want to defend and explain itself; it will try to correct what it perceives as a misrepresentation of what you did, and make it the director's/audience's failure to understand.

Meanwhile, you've totally missed the point of the critique or direction and cannot, or will not, make any adjustments that would actually serve you; your ego is in the way.

~~~~~~~~~~~~~~~~~~~~~~~~~~~~

Handling criticism from the perspective of self-esteem:

If you hear criticism or direction you're given from a place of self-esteem, you hear it very differently; in fact, you can actually *hear* it. You consider the critique as positive information that can help you to continue to grow and learn as a performer.

You're willing to listen to feedback; you're open to it being valid, valuable, and allow it to be a contribution to your advancement as an actor. You're able to discern between useful and non-useful information.

Taking direction becomes much easier and more fun. You hear direction, not as a put down of what you did, but as just another way of doing it. It allows you to be open to making the change easily and being excited about trying the suggestion. It leaves you feeling better about what you're doing, knowing that you've satisfied the director's request and your audience's enjoyment.

Oddly enough, even the high points of your career are handled differently by your ego and your self-esteem. For instance:

Handling acceptance from the ego's perspective:

It's strange that given the ego's job, it might have trouble with acceptance, but your ego may look at it as a *full course meal* to feed itself on, rather than the *a la carte* experience it should be.

The ego could be trying to hide your doubts and fears about not being good enough, using praise to cover them up, even though they exist deep down. At this point, one or more of the following happens when you are acknowledged and book a job:

-- Your ego takes it as proof – it needs proof – that you are indeed good enough. It allows the acceptance to go to your head, so to speak. It not only fiercely protects and defends it, but also blows it out of proportion. If and when that bubble bursts and the ego experiences rejection again, the crash back down to earth is so much more painful.

-- You might have such a swelled head you lose touch with reality and be in total denial of your need for growth and learning. This may result in stagnation of your creativity; you wonder why, if you're so good, you're still unemployed or you're employed but still miserable.

-- Your ego needs to pretend that the acceptance is proof of your worthiness, but believes deep down that you've fooled everyone into thinking you're good. Now the ego needs to work overtime to perpetuate the myth. This can result in your experiencing a great deal of stress and worry when you audition or work. You are hoping no one discovers the truth that you really aren't good enough, and praying that you can get away with it again.

~~~~~~~~~~~~~~~~~~~~~~~~~~~~~~

Handling acceptance from a place of self-esteem:

A high level of self-esteem is all-inclusive; it can manage acceptance the same way it deals with rejection because it knows there's nothing different about what you've done to deserve it – it's just your turn to be chosen, your turn to book the job. In fact you might have thought you weren't your best in that audition and you book the job anyway. So what? You know you can do well on the job. I've personally experienced that scenario more than once.

If you have self-esteem you also have room to be good and bad. You trust that both experiences are all in a day's work; you can really enjoy your acceptance, and celebrate your win, knowing it is fleeting and tomorrow you may be rejected again.

Your attitude on the job will be brighter as well. If you have confidence in your ability and it's finally been recognized, you'll look forward to the opportunity with less stress and pressure on having to prove your worth.

Handling praise from the ego's perspective:

From the ego's point of view receiving praise can be awkward and uncomfortable at best; at its worst, it actually doesn't *get it*.

If the ego sees 5 reviews and 4 of them are glowing but 1 of them is critical, all of the ego's attention is probably going to be on the critical one. You will either be thinking, "I didn't fool *that* one", or you will want to explain and defend yourself, feeling totally misrepresented by the critique.

If the ego hears praise regarding feedback from an audition, but you didn't book the job, there's a chance the ego will discount that feedback as meaningless. Since *the proof is in the booking* and you didn't book it, your ego still perceives it as a loss and ignores the win of the praise.

~~~~ Amazing, isn't it? ~~~~

Handling praise from a place of self-esteem:

From a place of self-esteem, praise can be accepted with grace and dignity. Criticism can be accepted as a learning tool.

If your self-esteem sees 5 reviews and 4 of them are glowing but 1 of them is critical, your attention will be distributed proportionately. You can allow the praise to sink in and celebrate it. You also have the opportunity to decide whether or not the critical one holds any value and contributes to your growth as a performer.

If you have self-esteem you're as comfortable with praise as you are with criticism and look at both sides as a learning experience. You have a better chance of seeing yourself as others see you; you can value their feedback whether it is positive or negative.

There is no right or wrong, good or bad.

There is just what is.

Balance is everything.

CHAPTER SIX

SUCCESS

This is a crazy business. It's difficult to define success when there are no clear rules to follow in order to achieve it. It's hard when, no matter what you do or how hard you work at it, producing successful results is out of your control.

Whatever your odds, chances are good that you'll be rejected more often than accepted. It's important that you measure your success on something other than booking the job.

Knowing that my odds are 1 in 10, I consider having an audition as being successful. I'm one step closer to booking a job. Every audition I do is at least practice and I take away another lesson from the experience. I call that being successful as well. These days, just being one of the six to twelve actors who get to audition should be considered success.

1. Healthy perspective

Since there are no guarantees in this business that you will ever reach your ultimate goal, it's really important that:

-- **You accept the reality of how this business works.** As if having to audition once or twice wasn't enough, there might be more hoops to go through. Even after the call back there may be a *third* audition, sometimes a *fourth* one and possibly a *screen test*.

If you make it that far, there are other stages in the casting process you might go through without even knowing about them. Your agent may not tell you as there is nothing more you need to do. It's in the producer's or network's hands.

You might be:

Short listed – they've narrowed the field and you're still in the running.

Down to two – it's between you and another actor. They haven't decided.

Pinned – your picture is up on the board with the other cast members, but they haven't booked you yet.

Waiting for network approval – they want you for the role, but if it's a network show, the network has final say.

At any one of these stages they may hire or eliminate you. Your agent may choose not to let you know until the final decision is made so you don't get your hopes up.

-- **You define success to include any progress you make.** Even if you don't book the job, consider any of these levels a major win. I know it can be devastating to have worked so hard, done so well, and gotten so close -- only to be told you didn't get it.

I know because I have been the queen of *short listing* for some time now. If I don't book it, my reaction ranges from mild disappointment to complete and utter meltdown, depending on how attached I've become to the role.

I've learned to let myself have whatever breakdown I need to have and then let it go. I try not to get too attached to any role so the letdown isn't as painful in case I don't get it. I'm not always successful with that one; but I've also learned to look on the bright side and remind myself that I was still:

-- One (out of many) who got a chance to read.
-- One (out of fewer) who got called back.
-- One (of only two or three) who made it to *serious consideration*.

If I make that win more important than the loss of the job, I'm in better shape to get out there and win the next time I have an audition.

-- **You set yourself up to win along the way.** The whole purpose of doing this is to offset the feeling of failure and rejection that so easily takes over if you aren't booking jobs. The win should be what you did to get as far as you have. It's the only thing you *deserve* credit for since that is in your control. You can't really take credit for *getting* the part. You haven't had anything to do with actually casting it, have you?

What you do with the results, good or bad, is also in your control. Find your balance in this area if you want a healthy, fulfilling and satisfying career. It's up to you.

If you let the rejections get you down, it will be harder to face new auditions with any self-esteem at all. If you let booking a job go to your head and then you don't book the next one, it will be all that much harder to take. Balance those highs and lows!

-- **You don't rely on this acting career to handle your financial needs and self-worth.** Unless you're on a series or you're independently wealthy, you have to handle your financial needs outside of your acting career. You cannot rely on acting as your sole source of income, even if you book jobs occasionally.

You never want to go into an audition being desperate because you can't pay your rent or bills. No matter how well you think you're hiding it, they can usually sense the desperation; even if they don't, you'll probably sabotage your performance with the amount of pressure you put on yourself *needing* this job.

It's okay to *want* the job — it's not okay to *need* it. Psychologically, there's a difference in the approach between those two things:

> -- If you want the job, it presumes the positive. You do your best and have fun with it, knowing this may be the only chance you get to perform this role. You do it for your audience's appreciation; whether you book it or not is irrelevant.

-- If you need this job, it presumes the negative. What you're probably thinking about is: not having a job, not having money, not being successful, not being good enough; and then you push and try too hard. You're thinking of all the things that you don't want to do wrong, which will be exactly what you create, because you're reinforcing the negative.

Here are some questions you should ask yourself. I understand that looking at the following can seem like messing with your dream, but it's actually necessary to help you achieve your dream.

-- Do I want to spend my life struggling to become a professional actor against overwhelming odds?

-- Do I want to rely on making it as an actor for my financial security and self-worth when chances are good I'll be living in poverty and misery?

-- What will *making it* look like?

-- What if I sacrifice everything and don't make it?

The standard in the acting profession seems to be luck, timing, contacts and a modicum of ability. As the statistics show, there are precious few who make a decent living from their acting careers. For the rest of us, acting is an expensive hobby with an occasional return on our investment. The best approach is to handle your financial security outside of this business, so you can *afford* to be an actor and enjoy pursuing your acting career. Here are other important questions to consider:

-- What else do I love to do?

-- How can I turn other things I love doing into a money making proposition?

-- Will it support my pursuing an acting career?

-- Can I do both while I wait to become a star?

-- You have another career that provides more success and security in your life. Many actors opt for a waiter/waitress job. Maybe it's the appeal of the job title – *wait*er, *wait*ress; while they *wait* to book an acting job.

Maybe it's perceived as the traditional route to take, as many actors have before them. Maybe it's a practical option, knowing that they must have a flexible work schedule *in case* an audition or job comes up. Maybe it's because they don't want to engage in another career that would distract them from pursuing their passion which is acting; so they take a waiter/waitress job, or any old job they can get, like it or not.

Whatever the reasoning, the truth is an actor has to work twice as hard as anyone else to handle financial security and pursue an acting career at the same time; as both careers require a good deal of time and attention.

If you're going to be working full time on a J-O-B as well as an acting career, why not look at other skills and interests you have that you might actually *enjoy* using in a J-O-B? In order to seriously consider this, you would have to take the blinders off of your one-track, acting career focus. You would have to allow yourself to look at other career options, as if an acting career isn't an option at all.

Wait! Don't panic! I'm not asking you to give up your acting career. I'm just asking you to look at what you would be doing with your life *if* acting wasn't an option. You can make *both* careers work but you have to seriously consider the other options first. What might stop you is the notion that if you allow yourself to look, you will be forfeiting your dream. That is just not true.

In fact, finding another career option answers the question, "What if I don't make it?" If you don't make it as an actor, you've still been successful, fulfilled and enjoyed financial security in your life. That's not the worst thing that could happen, is it?

Once you've allowed yourself to discover your other talents, abilities and interests, the only thing you need to address is how to make your other career work so it *supports* your dream profession. I call this process...

2. <u>The Entrepreneurial Actor</u>…Or…

"What else are you going to do while waiting to become a star?"

Years ago when I was acting/teaching in Los Angeles, I got tired of listening to bright, intelligent, creative actors asking if anyone knew of a waiter/waitress job because they needed one. They always sounded depressed when they talked about a J-O-B. I got to thinking there should be another way for these actors to support themselves doing something they *would enjoy doing* while they pursued their acting careers.

I created a program that allowed actors to explore their *other* talents and abilities so that they could come up with ways to financially support themselves doing something else they loved to do. I called this class *Creative Career Development*, but have recently changed the name to *The Entrepreneurial Actor*.

To my surprise, filling seats in this program was difficult. Getting actors to take a look at other career options was tricky. It made me realize how important and necessary it was. I finally gathered enough interest to run the course a couple of times.

I scoured self-help books and new age material. I found a variety of aptitude tests that were fun to do and used articles from banks on creating budgets and figuring out assets, liabilities and net worth. I wanted it to be a fun and informative self-exploration for each student; the only thing we could not talk about in class was *acting*!

The results of the course far exceeded my own expectations; not only did every student realize their other interests, but they also thought of ways to make their other career support their acting career. In fact, some realized they were more interested in their new career and gave up acting. For those students, acting had been more of a burden than a solution in their lives. Once they saw another path that excited them they were on it. By the end of the course, those students were happier and more excited than I had ever seen them before.

Out of all the students who went through it, there were only a couple whom I thought *had* to make it as actors; they had no other skills, aptitudes or interests, no matter what other options they explored.

I haven't done the course again since I left L.A. 25 years ago, but it's still on my mind and I'm thinking of offering it again. Nothing has changed for those pursuing an acting career; I actually think it's gotten tougher, as there are many more actors and fewer jobs.

Even for actors who appear to have a decent career, jobs can be few and far between. All the *smart* actors I know have figured out that they need another career, or at least realize that acting isn't their only interest.

When I started out it took a great deal of time, not to mention many J-O-B-S, to finally find my aptitude for and interest in teaching. For the majority of my career, I considered myself to be an *actress who taught*; it wasn't until recently that I realized I'm a *teacher who acts*. I've come to appreciate that and it doesn't take anything away from my passion for acting, which I still get to do every now and then.

I don't have to be one of the lucky ones to have figured that out. You can and *should* do it for yourself, too.

Following are some tips about exploring other career options, but first and foremost:

- You must take the blinders off.

- You must be willing to really look.

- You must allow yourself to explore your other abilities and interests.

- You must trust the process will support your dream career.

Creative Career Development tips:

-- Take a step back and look as objectively as you can at other options.

-- Pretend there is no such thing as an acting career; what would you do then?

-- Look at past jobs and volunteer work — which did you like doing and which did you hate doing?

-- Make a list of all your skills and hobbies. Which ones could lead to paying jobs?

-- Read some books on personal development about finding the right job, books on success and failure, etc.; there are tons of them out there. In my classes I used *WishCraft, What Color Is My Parachute*, and one of the original self-help books, *Psycho-cybernetics*.

-- Take some aptitude tests. There are some in *What Color Is My Parachute* and I'm sure there are many others available on line and in books of this genre.

-- Figure out what you need to earn to support your lifestyle. This will require you to do a budget and a financial worth report. I know this one's tough, but *do it*; get a grip on the reality of your situation.

-- Do some creative thinking *outside the box* about ways to generate an income.

-- Formulate a few options; eliminate what you aren't interested in doing from your field of choices, and seriously consider the ones that are left.

-- Look at how to work those options into alignment with your acting career. Which ones could you do that would *support* your dream career?

-- Put the wheels in motion; start taking *action* on one, or more, of those options and see if it can work for you.

If you're on the right path the universe will send you all kinds of support. If you're not, the universe will place obstacles in your way. Pay attention! If you're getting support, keep going. If you're coming up against obstacles, try a different path, but *don't give up*!

It's all in the *doing*; I'm a firm believer that if you take *action*, the universe responds with *action*. If you only t*hink about doing*, the universe supports your *thinking*; you have to make a move first. You'll find out soon enough if it was the right move or not.

When you get *active* the universe *re-acts*. I always say, "If you want to book a job plan a vacation". There's no better position to be in than win/win. If you get on with creating a successful life, instead of waiting around for your acting career to take off, you put yourself in that win/win situation.

If you've found a job that you love, it doesn't matter as much whether or not you book an acting job. If you do book one, you win; if you don't book, you win at being successful and happy in your other career. If you work things out well, you might just win at both!

As I said earlier, having two careers takes hard work. This is not a path for the *lazy* or *faint of heart*. If what I've said up until now makes you want to quit, then by all means quit; there's no shame in pursuing something, then realizing it's not for you. Talking someone out of an acting career is as much a success on my part as encouraging someone to do it, probably because I look at success and failure in a particular way.

3. Success vs. Failure

There are two sets of scenarios to look at in this area:
1. The short term success/failure *audition* story
2. The long term success/failure *career* story

1. Success/Failure Audition Story

The trick is to not base your success or failure booking the job; if you do, you will fail many more times than you will succeed. You're not going to book every audition you go on -- no one does. Actors who appear to work often probably do more auditions, or maybe their odds of booking are higher; but they still don't book every audition.

Even stars don't get every role they go after. There may be other stars the producers are interested in; or even if they don't have to audition, they are still only *under consideration* and might lose out to someone else. If there are four stars who would love to play the part, three of them aren't going to get the chance.

If you're like most actors who do have to audition, you need to base your success and failure on what you did, not on the outcome. You need to look at what went right/what went wrong in the audition and determine whether you succeeded in accomplishing what you set out to do.

Consider whatever you did right to be *a success* and whatever you did wrong to be a *lesson learned for next time*. These are results you can measure and are within your control to do something about.

Your mental state has a great deal to do with how you are performing. When you consider yourself successful you have confidence and do well. You probably won't do as well if you consider yourself a failure; so find success and/or learn the lesson in every audition you do. It'll do wonders for your self-worth and confidence to know that failure is not an option. There is only success and correction.

Be specific in your analysis of what worked/what didn't work in the audition. You can't fix *I suck*. You can fix *I wasn't listening*; I will listen better next time.

<u>A WORD OF CAUTION:</u> …regarding self-criticism…

I've learned that what we think or how we feel about what we did may have nothing to do with the outcome. You may think you were bad, but you book the job; or you may think you nailed it and you never hear from them again. It can be tough, but try to be as objective as possible when reviewing your work; remember, *no news is good news* regarding feedback from the casting directors.

2. <u>Success/Failure Career Story</u>

FAILURE

Let's deal with the nasty word first – failure. As I mentioned, rejection isn't necessarily a bad thing, neither is the idea of failure. It's our judgment of these concepts; what we think they mean and what we think they say about us that gives these words their negative connotation. It is how we hold it and what we do with the information that's important.

After all, there's only so much you can do to succeed as an actor. No matter how far you get or how far away you wind up, the only important question is…

"Did I do everything I could to get there?"

If the answer is "yes", then you've been successful. You just didn't get as far in your career as you had hoped you would, and it was not entirely in your control anyway.

Even if the answer is "no", it does not mean you have failed; it just gives you the opportunity to ge*t the lesson,* make necessary corrections, re-choose your goal, and move forward again. There's a great example of how this works in the book *Psycho-cybernetics.* It talks about how a guided missile finds its target. Once the missile is launched, it gets off its path and corrects back, gets off its path and corrects back until it reaches its destination. In other words, it fails…corrects, and fails…corrects, until it succeeds.

We can learn from this example: *Success is just a series of failures that get corrected.* You must be willing to fail in order to be successful. Failure is not something to fear if you consider it a step on the road to success.

As I've mentioned in an earlier section, there's a difference between how the professional actor looks at failure, and how a newcomer views it.

-- <u>Newcomers are trying hard not to fail or make a mistake. They're trying to look professional.</u> Trying hard not to fail makes them tense, work too hard and play it safe. It keeps their mind on the negatives of what could go wrong and makes them more worried and nervous. It makes them look *green* (like beginners).

-- <u>Professionals have learned from experience there's a good chance they will make mistakes; they have learned to recover and keep going.</u> Working with this attitude makes them less worried and more relaxed. They're willing to take risks, and are fearlessly daring. There's less pressure to get it right and they're able to have more fun.

The only real failure is in letting failure stop you:
- from pursuing your dream,
- from learning the lesson,
- from making correction and moving forward again.

The only real failure is in not recognizing the truth about your *willingness* to do what it takes to have a career. It may be that you are not willing, but you tell yourself (and everyone else) that you are. You blame your failure on circumstances or other people and wonder why you're not getting anywhere in your career.

If you get stuck you may need to re-evaluate your situation and make a decision about whether this career is right for you. As I've said, there's no shame or failure in trying this career out and then realizing it's not for you It's better to admit it, find a more suitable career and be happy, than it is to lie to yourself and everyone else and be miserable.

I also hear actors say...

"I'm afraid of failing. That's why I'm stuck and can't move forward in my career."

It could be true, but I'll bet it's more a *fear of success* that's stopping them; so let's look at "success"...

...FAILURE is easy...

...It's SUCCESS that's hard...

We're comfortable more with failure than we are with success; it is familiar territory, odd as that may sound. We tried, we failed – end of story; pressure is off. We get to start all over again and as soon as it gets *uncomfortable*, we fail again.

But success is trickier; when we begin to experience some success, we are in new territory. There's more at stake, greater responsibility, and more stress and pressure; we are out of our comfort zone. It's not surprising that there is an instinctive fear of it.

SUCCESS

Okay! You book the job! Congratulations! Now the real work begins.

I always say that the most enjoyable time for me is *between* booking the job and doing the job. It's when I get to enjoy my success the most. As soon as I have to do the job, the pressure is on again. Now there's even more at stake; they are paying me to produce results, to be good at what I do, to be professional, to get it *right*.

It does get a bit easier once you've been through a few bookings, but every job is different; it's as if you're starting over with each one.

Booking your first acting job presents a whole new learning curve. In fact, there's enough new information about working on set to warrant a sequel to this book. Most successful actors learn the ropes by jumping in, figuring it out as they work, and consider it *on-the-job training*.

Being successful brings up a whole new set of issues to deal with, and the more successful you become the greater the challenges you will face.

Here are some things you will have to consider now that you have been *successful* at booking a job...

> ➢ Will I ever book another one?
> ➢ Can I get to larger, better roles?
> ➢ Will I be as good or better in the next role?
> ➢ How do I advance my career now?

If you're fortunate enough to book something really big, a series regular or a major motion picture, life gets even more complicated; ask anyone who's been there.

You'll be dealing with...

> ➢ Press events
> ➢ Publicity tours
> ➢ Charities who come begging
> ➢ Public attention (paparazzi, fans, etc.)
> ➢ Pressure of being responsible for the success of the project
> ➢ Moving up to a new level of competition for roles
> ➢ Concern for keeping your career status

... On and on it goes... No wonder we fear success!

If you're one of those people who pictures success as sitting by the pool sipping a drink, one of those actors who thinks that once you make it life will get easier, *think again*. If you look at being successful as an opportunity to take on greater challenges, look forward to having more responsibility and working harder than ever, you have a chance to enjoy a successful career.

All the glamour and the perks will have been well earned. What might appear as *star treatment* is really a necessity more than a luxury given the schedules and demands placed on you, the actor.

It's no wonder that some successful actors resort to drugs, alcohol and even suicide; they may have been among those who didn't know what success would really look like.

There are also stars who realize that *star power* isn't totally satisfying because it doesn't give them control over their projects and careers. Even though they are successful, they are still not feeling fulfilled. They turn to directing, producing, forming their own production companies, or going into some other business. In short, being successful isn't always what it's cracked up to be.

There's also the issue of maintaining a successful career. Again, there are no guarantees. Actors can have good years and bad years. They can book 10 jobs in one year and not book one job the next. They might land a series-regular role and the show gets cancelled after one season.

Given the nature of this business, no matter what level of success you experience, it's always a good idea to have some other source of interest and income to fall back on. My last piece of advice to you is...

4. Don't quit your day job.

Until you're making a substantial living as an actor and you have so many job offers coming your way you have no time for anything else, don't give up your day job!.

Hopefully you've got another career you enjoy and can look forward to doing again if you're out of work as an actor. Certainly, in the early stages of a career making a decent living as an actor is iffy at best.

Even if it looks as if you're on your way, your status could literally change overnight; so don't be too quick to abandon your other sources of income. If you've been smart, you've set yourself up in another career that you can leave for a period of time, but go back to whenever necessary.

That's why so many actors *create their own* businesses that they can:
1) rely on a staff to run, while they work as actors.
2) pick up and do again whenever they have time.
3) draw some salary from if they are not present.
4) work at even while working as actors.

If you should be so lucky as to reach the level of making a substantial living in your dream profession, it's still wise to save some of that income towards investing in your retirement, or towards investing in a different career should you tire of acting or the acting business tires of you.

I have had what some would call a moderately successful acting career. I have a fairly substantial resume which I add to every now and then; but while most people my age are enjoying retirement, I'm still looking for a job and having to fall back on my teaching career, creating my own classes and workshops or teaching at an acting school. It's a good thing I love what I do and have no real desire to retire.

Although I have had many opportunities as an actress, I've never given up my teaching/coaching career. In fact, I think I'd give up acting before I'd quit teaching. I have frequently contemplated doing just that, but then I wouldn't know what was going on in the world of auditioning. My teaching has actually kept me in the acting game.

For the last few years I've been lucky enough to have worked full time on a popular TV series as a coach and still been able to do the occasional acting job. I say that I've been lucky; but I've also worked hard at setting up my careers and juggling them all, so I can maintain my particular lifestyle.

You can do it too. If you have a burning desire to make it work and are willing to do what it takes, the universe will respond with support.

CHAPTER SEVEN

ON TRAINING: CLASSES and WORKSHOPS

I'm reluctant to get into this area because I am a teacher and have a very strong, subjective opinion about where actors should be spending what little money they have on classes. However, it's such an integral part of an actor's career I feel I must cover some aspects of it. I will deal with this as objectively as I can.

1. <u>What kind of classes to take</u>:

If you are just dabbling in acting and not seriously considering an acting career, take any type of class that interests you and would be fun. It's a great place to work on self-expression, emotional connection, and communication skills.

If you are serious about an acting career, I suggest you give more thought to what skills you'll need for your advancement. Look to areas of weakness in your skill set, not your areas of strength; take classes that will improve those skills and be willing to learn. Don't take classes to show everyone what you already know.

Basic acting, voice and movement are a must; a good foundation of training will stand you in good stead for all types of work. Also consider training specifically for the medium of acting you are most interested in pursuing.

For example:
-- If you want to do **theatre/stage** work, take basic acting, scene study, and voice and movement classes.

-- If you want to do **commercials**, take a Commercial Audition Technique class. There's more to learn than you might think about commercial auditions. They are unique and require a different skill set than any other type of audition.

-- If you want to do **film and TV**, take classes that specifically work with on-camera skills. It's quite different than working on stage.

-- If you want to do **voice-over**, then take classes that train you "on mic" in all aspects of voice work: cartoon/animation, commercial/PSA spots, narration, and dubbing.

Each performing medium requires a different skill set, so find the classes that specialize in the areas of your interests. You don't have to take them all at once. Pace yourself. It's a good idea to focus on one area then move on to another. In some cases, the techniques are so different you don't want to confuse yourself trying to learn both at the same time.

If you are interested in more than one area, I suggest you focus first on the classes that will help you make a return on your investment. For instance, it's not a good idea to take a class in Shakespeare if you are headed for doing film and TV. It wouldn't hurt to do that, but it won't help either, especially if you don't know how to audition for film and TV yet.

If you are not sure of which avenue you want to pursue, then find a few short-term classes that give you some experience in each area to help you get clearer on what suits your talents and interests best.

If you have trained extensively and are working professionally, it is still a good idea to continue working out in a class situation. At this point, take whatever you like, but keep those juices flowing.

SPECIAL NOTE:

All actors need to train in voice and movement even if they are only interested in film and TV. You need to know how to breathe, project, develop vocal stamina and control, be aware of your body and use it effectively. This training can also help you learn how to release emotionally; yes, it is all necessary even in film!

2. How to choose a class:

As I've said, focus on the area you are most interested in first. Find the instructors who *specialize* in that area and narrow down the field of teachers.

Do your research:

-- Check the credentials of the teacher. You can get information on the Internet about them: International Movie Database (IMDb) most likely will have their work history, or *Google* their name.

-- Check out their reputation with others. Ask other performers, agents, and casting directors for their opinions.

-- Audit their class. Most teachers allow one free audit. Meet them, watch how they work. Ask questions.

-- Check out more than one. Every teacher's style is different and you should be able to make a comparison; whom can learn from and whom will be an inspiration to you.

Choose wisely

I suggest you base your ultimate decision on whom you think will be best suited for your needs:

-- If you are an overly sensitive type, you may need the teacher who is gentle in his/her approach.

-- If you thrive on being pushed, then go with the tough love teacher.

-- Just make sure you trust them and are willing to grow and learn from them.

Buyer Beware! If you are considering a full-time acting program, check the credentials of the *individual* teachers as well as the school's overall reputation. They may be charging more than what the quality of training is worth. Think carefully about student loan debt; there is little or no assurance you'll be able to repay that loan with acting work.

3. **What NOT to take:**

-- <u>Don't take classes that aren't applicable to your area(s) of interest:</u>
For instance:
-- If you are interested in commercials, don't take scene study; it won't help you audition for commercials.
-- If you are only interested in film and TV, don't take a class in commercials; they are very different mediums.
-- If you are only interested in stage, don't take an on-camera class; the logistics and levels of performance are quite different.

As I've said, once you are proficient in your primary area of interest, you can take anything you like, but first focus on the one area you intend to work in the most.

-- <u>Don't take Casting Director Workshops until you are confident you can impress them.</u>
All actors want to meet Casting Directors. When you are just starting out it may be harder and take longer than you expect to get in to see them. You might decide to take their workshop and meet them that way, but before you jump in, please consider the following:
-- Although they say they understand you are in training and they are just teaching, are you sure they will bring you in to audition even if you don't impress them in the workshop?
-- Are you willing to risk the chance that they won't see you for a very long time, even if you have gotten better since taking the workshop?
-- Do you really want to spend your money on possibly *damaging* your chances of being seen by that casting director?
-- Are you really confident that you can impress them, no matter how pressured you feel or nervous you are?
-- Can you take their directions and not let them throw you?
-- Are you really ready to *knock their socks off*?

If the answer is "yes" to all of those questions, then by all means do it. If the answer is "no", then hold off until you are ready. It's also a good idea to let your agent do what he/she can to get you in first. If that fails and you are really ready, then maybe you should take their workshop.

I do know that after doing their workshop actors have impressed them and get called in to audition, when before they couldn't get in to see them. Just be sure you are on your game if you do take a Casting Director Workshop.

-- <u>Don't do Star Search, Talent Scout Contests:</u>
These people usually come from out-of-town. They charge a hefty fee and your chances of being discovered are slim to none, particularly if you are an actor. They might be doing the search to enroll you in something that costs even *more* money, and the prize might sound way better than it actually is.

-- If it is a Modeling/Talent Search, they may give out a couple of modeling contracts, but as for the talent search, don't count on winning as your big break: the best you can hope for is probably advice from the panel of judges.
-- If you have money to burn and you want the experience, then do it. But don't have high expectations.
-- If there is a Casting Call for a specific project in your area, it might be more legitimate and worth going to, and it should not cost money to do it.

-- <u>Don't take a class because your agent says you must or they won't take you on.</u>
If it is a class offered by an agency, the agency may be making most of its money from classes and not by getting their clients work. I wouldn't sign with that agent. If it's a class offered outside of the agency, the agent may be getting a commission (kickback) from the teacher for enrollments and may be more interested in that than in finding the *right* class for you. If an agent recommends more than one teacher, or hosts a one-time workshop for their clients, that's okay; have a look at those classes and decide for yourself.

4. <u>How long should you study?</u>

Basically, the answer is *forever*. You are never really finished training. Is a dancer, singer, musician ever finished practicing? Unless you are quite disciplined and practice on your own at least a few times a week, you need to be in a class. If you are working constantly you are still training, you're just doing it on-the-job.

-- <u>You have to train until you know you are proficient in the area of study.</u>
It usually takes longer than you would like it to take. There may be steps forward and then steps backward for a while. Don't quit. Keep going until you feel confident with your skills and it is reflected in your feedback from teachers and other professionals.

Once you are proficient in that area, you can move on to expand your expertise in other areas, get into a maintenance workout class, or study different approaches in the same area of study. For instance:

--you've taken basic acting courses for a while; move on to scene study, or audition technique.

--you've taken audition technique courses; then move on to scene study.

--you've taken commercial audition technique courses; so move on to an improvisation class.

--you've taken scene study and audition technique, and you're interested in studying Shakespeare; then do it.

--you've studied with the same teacher for years. Try someone else.

--you've studied a particular Technique (like Meisner). Try a different one.

Always be willing to get out of your comfort zone and try something new. If you're a working actor and your skill is in good shape, but singing terrifies you – take a singing class.

Keep stretching and growing And remember to always be willing to learn, no matter how often you work, or how long you've been in the business.

5. The misconception:

I've heard so many actors say that business is slow so there's no need to study right now. That's just *wrong*.

In fact, that is the time to make sure you are continually working out so when business picks up and auditions start coming you are ready to kick butt, as the saying goes.

I've had actors come to me in a panic because they *finally* have an audition and need coaching. When we start working on the scene, I can tell they are rusty, or they have forgotten their basic preparation tools. Well, it's too late now. I can't fix everything in an hour that I see needs some tuning up.

Knowing the answer already, I ask them if they've been studying. The reply is usually the same, "No, it's been so slow!" For some it's actually been a year or longer since they've taken a class.

You don't want to be doing your tune up in an actual audition. You always want to be ready to go at a moment's notice on a regular basis. I don't care if it's been two years since you had an audition; all the more reason to have been studying -- that is, if you want to work!

Afterword

So, there you have it! Audition Technique as I've understood and been teaching it these many years. I'm not one to drop names, so I'll just say that I have had many students who have gone on to have very successful careers. You might not recognize all of their names, but they are working actors who make a living in this business. I'm proud to say I've also trained a few actors who have gone on to become excellent teachers in their own right.

I may not see or hear from some students for years; but when our paths cross once again, I'm reminded of the impact my classes have had on them. At the same time, they have all made a huge contribution to my development of this technique with their hard work and feedback, for which I am very grateful. They are the inspiration for this book.

My purpose in teaching this technique has always been so that actors could prepare their own auditions, and not have to rely on getting coached for every role. Yes, coaching may be necessary for certain roles: when the scenes are logistically difficult, or the actor just can't figure out the material. It's smart to get help; but coaching is expensive. Why not develop the confidence that you can handle it yourself, look great and have fun?

Some actors need to rely on their acting coach for almost everything. That's fine if they have the financial resources. I think some coaches help to create this kind of dependency, but that's not my style. I'm more interested in developing self-sufficient actors who are confident with their technique.

Some well-known actors have said that if they had to audition they wouldn't work very often; others have said they don't audition, not because they feel they're above it, but because they're too scared and hate having to face them. I hope this book helps give you more confidence than that!

Michael Shurtleff's book, *Audition*, has become something of an actor's bible. Almost every actor I know has a copy – even if they haven't read it yet. I still to this day recommend it to my students as #1 on my book list. It has helped me tremendously in formulating my auditioning for film technique. After all these years of teaching the technique, his recommendations and insights still hold up; but now that I've written *this* book, I like to think of Mr. Shurtleff's as the *Old Testament* and this as the *New Testament*.

I hope this book has clarified the elements of the process and will be a reference guide when you have an audition to prepare or you're just practicing. I do encourage you to take classes though. Nothing can take the place of actually getting on your feet and *doing* it.

I also hope that my suggestions for handling this business as a career choice and for maintaining a healthy psychological perspective will be of help as well. I'm a firm believer that you can have it all – if you are willing to work hard enough.

Special note to teachers: If you find value in these pages for your students, please use it with my blessing. If you encourage them to buy a copy, thank you!

Good luck. Bonne chance. Break a leg!

Linda Darlow

Index

Index

Index

CPSIA information can be obtained
at www.ICGtesting.com
Printed in the USA
BVHW010603020721
610928BV00013B/99

9 781460 220757